Children's talks with puppet sketches 2

John Hardwick

kevin
mayhew

First published in 2004 by

KEVIN MAYHEW LTD
Buxhall, Stowmarket, Suffolk, IP14 3BW
E-mail: info@kevinmayhewltd.com

9 8 7 6 5 4 3 2 1 0

ISBN 1 84417 325 9
Catalogue No. 1500741

Edited and typeset by Graham Harris
Cover design by Angela Selfe

Printed and bound in Great Britain

Contents

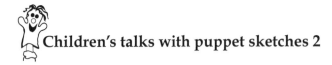

Dedication

This book is dedicated to my father, Leslie Hardwick, and my late mother, Ruth Hardwick, who since long before I was born were involved in reaching out to children through Sunday school, midweek children's club and a beach mission at Skegness, Lincolnshire. They helped me see the importance of reaching children who often have little knowledge of the Bible or of God's love for them.

I'd especially like to thank my wife Rachel, daughter Chloe and son Ben for their love and support.

John Hardwick

Foreword

John Hardwick is one of those unique individuals who somehow seems to have received more than his fair share of gifts! It is something I know only too well, after working alongside John for a number of years.

Through that time I am pleased that I learnt a great deal from him, so I am especially glad that some of that experience and expertise is passed on through this book.

John's ability to communicate creatively, added to his love for the Bible, and his passion for reaching children of all ages for Jesus, mean that this new book is one that I am sure will enhance the work that you do to share God's good news.

Alan Charter
Head of Missions, Scripture Union
207-209 Queensway
Bletchley, Milton Keynes
MK2 2EB
Tel: 01908 856125

Why use puppets?

What people say about puppets!

'A visual aid you can use time after time!'

'A visual aid children will ask you about, even when it's not in use!'

'A friend for life'

'Easy to use'

'Appeals to all ages!'

'Relatively cheap'

'Wonderful for introducing and illustrating themes!'

'There's one out there somewhere, just waiting for you! A style and a puppet to suit you!'

Variety of puppets

At some stage we have all enjoyed watching puppets in action. Puppets can be simple or complex! Sooty and Sweep, Thunderbirds, The Muppets, Spitting Image, ventriloquist dolls/puppets – such a variety, yet all have made their mark in the entertainment world.

Grabs people's attention!

Just sitting in a room with a cuddly toy on your lap looking at people guarantees that you will become the centre of attention! Children love to watch puppet shows. Ventriloquists are often included in variety shows. Very few art forms can capture the imagination of adults and children in one single performance, which is why ventriloquists often do well in talent shows.

A friend for life

Unlike many tricks or visual aids, you can use your puppet time after time. It becomes a real friend to the children, someone they can relate to. When I'm out and about I often have children come up to me wanting to see Micky (my monkey puppet), asking where he is and what he's up to. He's even been on the front pages of newspapers, opened school halls and been asked to cut the ribbon! I've even had headteachers asking if Micky could go and take their school assembly!

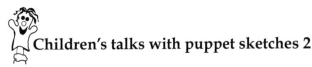

A solo performer becomes a double act!

You may be in a situation where you present a children's talk or lesson on your own. For example, you might be a church minister or speaker, a Sunday school teacher or a school teacher. This can be limiting when it comes to trying to put across a message in a creative way, time after time.

A puppet is like having an acting partner, someone to perform sketches with and bounce lines off. It's another personality or character! The advantage is they are able to practise when it suits you, so you don't have to find a time to suit both diaries!

Puppets can be very childlike or innocent in their under-standing. They get into all kinds of situations and get away with things that human speakers cannot!

For example, Micky often starts a sketch by going to have a closer look at the audience and then announces that he feels very much at home among so many monkeys!

More than just entertainment!

Puppets are a wonderful teaching aid. Children seem to relate easily to the puppet – they're often more prepared to listen to a puppet than to a human.

Puppets often get things wrong and mess up or say the wrong thing! They may not understand something, and they get confused and upset. By explaining something to the puppet you're also reaching the audience, but in a non-threatening way! Children don't feel 'got at' but they get the message loud and clear! Puppets can introduce, illustrate, or reinforce themes.

Ideal for:

- Children's/all-age talks in church services
- Primary school assemblies
- Sunday schools or midweek children's programmes
- Open-air activities

I often use mine with older people, too. Micky is well-known at several retirement homes and women's meetings.

Writing a script

When people first handle a puppet they normally just look around at people or start to batter people with it!

However, coming up with a script is relatively easy. With time, practice and imagination you'll be amazed by what you come up with.

Look at your audience

If the majority of your audience are children then try to think through what a child's daily routine might be like.

Generalise a little! Older children may like to stay in bed, while younger ones often wake the house up. Girls may spend ages brushing their hair, boys don't bother (or is it the other way round?)

What might they have for breakfast? What do they like or dislike? Favourite or least favourite food, game, television programme, subject at school, pop star/group, football team, etc.

All of these areas could be used in a puppet sketch and will hold the children's attention because they want to know the puppet's favourite and you will be including things which mean a lot to the children.

Use everyday situations

Think of things from your childhood that made you happy or upset you. For example:

- being the person who isn't picked for a team!
- being the smallest person
- your first day at school
- how you felt when someone broke something you made
- being chosen for something
- winning a competition

Current events

Think of things you may be up to now!

When I was decorating a room at home I thought to myself: 'I wonder what a room would look like if it had been decorated by my puppet!?'

Keep it down to earth

The puppet is not the vicar, minister, preacher or worship leader.

It's not advisable for them to pray, preach the sermon, give their testimony, baptise, or take funeral services! However, they could interview people (although some of the more serious spiritual questions could be asked by another interviewer).

They could give out the weekly notices, but not the serious ones such as praying for those who are sick, or even those who are sick of the church!

A fast-moving visual aid

Their main strength is illustrating, introducing, reinforcing a point or a theme!

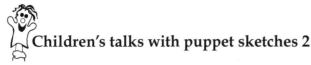

Using Bible stories

Don't come up with a puppet sketch and then try to find a Bible story that you could make fit your theme! You must work the other way round, keeping true to the Word of God. Choose a Bible story or passage and then come up with a sketch to help illustrate its teaching!

Using cuddly toys or wooden spoons with faces

You may have simple props such as cuddly toys or even wooden spoons. You could put up a screen and use the puppets to act out the story as a narrator tells or reads the story. You could have different people with different voices for each of the cuddly toys/actors!

Using other fables and other stories

Many children's stories and fables bring out good morals. You can easily adapt these for puppet sketches.

Using backing music and backing vocals

Puppets miming along to songs can be very effective and also very funny.

For example, a tiny mouse puppet singing opera will grab people's attention.

Puppets performing raps! Including the cool shades!

A team of puppets singing and swaying to a gospel song.

You can even get tapes with puppets in dialogue so all you have to do is mime along! (If pop stars can get away with it then why not puppets!)

Endless variety and styles

There really is 'something for everyone' when it comes to puppets, so go on – give them a go!

Styles –

Puppet to human

A dialogue between a puppet and the operator

The whispering puppet

The puppet pretends to talk to the operator (e.g. whispering in the operator's ear) This is relatively simple yet very effective.

Wonderful for if you are a solo worker because you have another character to bounce lines off and to do sketches with.

You are not stuck behind a puppet theatre or screen, so it's easy to have good interaction with the audience. In fact you can go right up to them and even pick on an individual (e.g. if someone sneezes in the audience it's easy for the puppet to look directly at that person and say 'bless you!' – always gets a laugh!)

You don't have to cart round any theatre or screen. Just a simple bag, box, basket, small dustbin or case!

It's amazing how excited the children become when they recognise the bag. Therefore, be careful in the way you handle it, it's carrying a precious cargo!

Getting started

The sketch starts as soon as you pick up the bag. I often say something like: 'I've brought along a friend of mine', and while I'm saying this I pick up the bag, undo the zip a little way, and start to put my hand inside the puppet while it's still in the bag. It's important to have the puppet the right way round in the bag so that the bottom of the puppet is close to where the bag starts to open.

If the puppet is in a box, have a hole at the back of the box so that your arm goes through the hole straight into the puppet!

When your arm is right inside the puppet and able to operate the mouth, open the rest of the zip and then let the puppet peep out, looking at the audience. Encourage the puppet to come right out. 'Come on, Micky, they're waiting for you.' The mood the puppet's in determines the speed he comes out of the bag. I normally put my other hand under the puppet as though it's taking the weight, because it helps to hide the fact that your other hand is inside the puppet. And now you are ready to proceed with the sketch!

Whispering techniques

As the puppet whispers in your ear relay what the puppet is saying to the audience.

At other times the puppet can whisper and you just nod, keeping the audience in suspense! You and the puppet may choose to look at someone and pretend to have a private conversation, both looking at the person, then at each other, shaking your heads or laughing. The audience will be longing to know what you are saying.

You can also have the puppet whisper a long sentence into your ear and then you relay a very short sentence. This always gets a laugh!

Since you are translating what the puppet is saying you will have to adapt the wording of the scripts in the book in places!

For example, if the script says 'I want to go for a walk' as the puppet whispers in your ear you will say, 'You want to go for a walk' Changing 'I' to 'You'. You'll soon get the hang of it!

Character

Give your puppet a character. It may be cheeky, a comedian, eager to learn or a bit of a 'know it all'. Shy or an extrovert, sporty or lazy, agreeing with everything you say or arguing every point!

The character may be shaped by what the puppet is or looks like.

For example, if it's a monkey puppet, monkeys are generally cheeky and full of excitement.

Movement

Remember that the puppet must come across as being alive. When I first take Micky out of his bag he has a look around to see where he is. Something may catch his eye so when I'm trying to talk to him he's not taking a scrap of notice! He may then start to chat about what he has seen and I try to get him to listen to me!

He will react if there is a background noise or a sudden movement nearby. He may shake with fear and hide his face in my shoulder as I comfort him and assure him it's quite safe. Sometimes we fall out and every time I look at him he looks away. Then I look away so he looks at me, then as soon I as look at him again he looks away!

When he's happy his movement is quick and excitable. He even jigs around, he calls it dancing. When he's sad his movement is slow and solemn!

Facial expression

Some puppets have soft faces, which means you are able to pull faces. A puppet pulling a face always gets a reaction!

Practise!

Practise in front of a mirror, because this helps you see what works and what doesn't work. Practise movement, whispering technique, the way you react with the puppet, pulling faces and sketches.

Sketches

With this style of puppet don't worry about knowing the sketch off by heart. After all, it's only you who knows if you didn't get it word perfect! Read the sketch over and over again. Try and remember the main points and the good jokes. Then you will have fun and be flexible enough to react to the audience. The secret is to read it over and over again until it really sinks in and then you'll find the sketch will flow!

The end!

Don't finish a sketch with you and the puppet falling out! The children may choose to side with the puppet! If the puppet has done something wrong then the sketch normally ends with the puppet going off to put it right, finishing on a positive note rather than a negative one. The puppet will then say goodbye and disappear into its bag. Never just leave a puppet on the side, out and in full view – it will have no life and will ruin what you have just done – and some children can be upset!

After the sketch

Children or adults may ask if they can have a go with your puppet! I always say no, because the puppet's character will not be the same, once again ruining what you have just done!

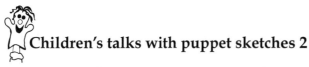

You may choose to get the puppet out to show them again, otherwise just say that the puppet is asleep or can become grumpy when disturbed, or he's just too busy!

You can do it!

I believe that with a little practice anyone can learn to use a puppet in this way. Go for it and you'll have a wonderful visual aid and a friend for life!

Styles –

Puppet to puppet

Puppet talk

There are several different styles and methods enabling the puppets to communicate with the audience.

A dialogue between the puppets
Puppets chatting to each other with the operator(s) being hidden behind a black cloth in a puppet theatre or behind a screen.

Puppets in dialogue with each other will require plenty of practice. If there are two or more operators then you need to know your script, otherwise you will talk over the top of each other.

A single operator can work both puppets in a puppet theatre. This also requires plenty of practice! Having a different puppet on each arm with each having its own voice and personality is quite a challenge at first, as you strive to make sure that you don't get the two mixed up! This style may sound too difficult, but I know several people who have picked this up relatively quickly!

Operating the puppet(s)

Position of the puppet
It is important for the puppet to look as though it is real and alive! Therefore the position of the puppet is very important!

- Make sure the puppet is upright and not leaning to one side.
- Make sure the puppet is looking where it's meant to be looking and not up at the ceiling or floor! If it's having a conversation with the audience then look at the audience and not above their heads or at their feet. This will take practice so ask someone to watch to help you get it right!
- Do move the puppets! Turn their heads to look at each other. If they are excited, jig them around. If they are sad their movement is slower and they will look down!

Mouth movement

When we talk we start with the mouth closed and then open and close it for the different syllables and words.

However, when people first try to speak with a puppet they start with the mouth open and close and open it for each word – the wrong way round!

- Start with the mouth closed then push the mouth open and closed to form the different words.
- Try and keep the puppet's top lip fairly still so you are moving mainly your thumb (in the lower part of the mouth) to create the words.
- Don't concentrate so hard on the script that you forget to move the mouth when talking. This looks rather odd!
- If you are using two puppets, make sure you use the right voice with the right puppet!

The voice

Try to develop a voice for the puppet that is different from your own. It may be higher or lower in pitch, depending on the gender or age of the puppet character. You could try an accent e.g. a country accent, Scottish, Welsh, Irish, Yorkshire, Birmingham, Cockney, French, American, or a posh English accent etc.

The character

Choose a name and a character style to suit your puppet and stick to it. For example, the puppet could be quiet and shy, confident and an extrovert, an intelligent thinker, a bit of a lad, bossy, mean, crazy, cheeky. Think about the age of the puppet. Is it a child, teenager, adult, old person?

- What sort of voice would they have?
- What is important to them and what would their conversation be about?
- Where do they go and what do they do during the day?
- Would they listen to One FM, Radio Four, Classic FM or none of them?
- Would they watch TV soaps, the news, children's TV, sport, documentaries?

Some Do's and Don'ts

Do

   . . . know what you are going to say, and be very familiar with the outline and the point of the sketch.

   . . . practise! You could do so in front of the mirror, which is really helpful.

   . . . speak clearly!

   . . . look in the right direction and not at the ceiling or down at the floor!

   . . . use humour.

   . . . have a go.

Don't

   . . . try and keep the puppet up too long, because your arms will tire very quickly.

   . . . forget to move the mouth when you talk.

   . . . use the wrong voice for the puppet.

   . . . show a dead puppet! (a puppet left out for all to see)

   . . . be put off when it doesn't go quite as well as you hoped!

. . . And do have fun!

Styles –

The puppet theatre

The puppet theatre is an ideal way for the operator to be hidden from the audience while still providing the opportunity to see a little of the audience and therefore have interaction. It also means that the operator's arms are bent and tucked into their body, giving some useful support. However, space inside the puppet theatre is limited.

Puppet theatres can be difficult to transport from place to place.

Styles –

A puppet screen

A puppet screen can either be a frame with a cloth covering or a more solid piece of hardboard fixed to a frame.

They can be any size, often depending on the size of your car!

You can paint all kinds of designs on these. The hardboard screens are easy to cut and therefore can be turned into wonderful sets such as a castle or a ship, or you can let your imagination run wild! Very visual, attracting attention!

You can have several operators behind one screen.

However, the operator normally has their arms outstretched above their heads, so this becomes tiring after a short while. It's also very difficult to interact with the audience. The staging and number of puppets can work out quite expensive, but remember you can use puppets over and over again. You can use these in church services, schools and they are a wonderful attraction in the open air.

A team of puppeteers can come up with some wonderful ideas and become close friends!

Sketches –

Off you go!

The following pages include sketches which I have used with Micky the monkey. I have written them as I perform them with him, but you can easily adapt them to your situation and your puppet. It's really important to rehearse and practise as much as possible, so that you can relax and not worry about delivering the script word perfect.

Eye contact between you and your puppet, you and the audience and the puppet and the audience are important, so that they forget the fact that the puppet is actually being controlled by you and believe he has a life of his own.

Autumn delights

 Aim
The different seasons are like different stages in people's lives. Each is valuable and has its own beauty.

Songs

Variety, variety (*Come On, Let's Celebrate*)
Anytime, anywhere (*Come On, Let's Celebrate*)
Never, never, never (*Come On, Let's Celebrate*)
Be kind and compassionate (*Bible Explosion*)

Puppet sketch

Micky	I was playing hide and seek with my friends. I climbed up my favourite tree, but they found me straight away because all the leaves had fallen off.
John	That's because it's autumn. Leaves fall off the trees to make space for new life, which will arrive in the spring.
Micky	I wish it was always summertime – always hot and I would be able to play outside.
John	The earth needs the different seasons and each season has its own beauty. It's nice having the variety. Like, in winter I know you love playing out in the snow. You can't do that in summer!
Micky	Oh, yeah! I love sledding and throwing snowballs!
John	Yes and in spring I can remember how excited you were!
Micky	Oh, yeah! Wherever I looked there were thousands of flowers.
John	The different seasons remind me of different stages in people's lives. Spring reminds me of new life . . .
Micky	(*Interrupting*) Like me! Young and full of life!
John	Yes! Full of bounce, energy and enthusiasm, discovering and learning . . . Full of excitement and fun. So you're at the 'spring' stage of life – we need people like you. Then comes summer. In summer we tend to slow down a bit!
Micky	Like you.
John	Thanks a lot! But you're probably right. I'm at the 'summer' stage of life – stronger, with plenty of ideas and I get things done. Then comes autumn. What does autumn remind you of, Micky?
Micky	Leaves falling off my favourite tree!

John	Yes, trees are solid and they've been around a long time. They've seen a lot and learnt a lot. Like older people. They've been around a long time, and they've seen a lot and learnt a lot. They have plenty of life experience. Then there's winter – a time when the earth rests and many animals hibernate – have a sleep.
Micky	That's a good idea! I could do with a nap! (*Micky yawns and leaves*)

Bible story

One of the most famous people in the Bible is David! When he was a boy he was a shepherd looking after his father's sheep, but God noticed him and saw that he was a good, kind boy who really cared for his sheep. God decided that one day he would make this shepherd boy king! He knew that he would really care for the people just like he cared for his sheep.

He was a bit of a pop star, and the king himself would ask for David to play his harp for him. It must have been strange, knowing that one day he would take over and become the new king – but he decided to keep quiet about that one!

When he was a teenager he was the only one brave enough to fight against a nasty giant. He put his trust in God and God gave him the victory! When David was a man he finally became the king. He was a good king who was kind, even to the last king's family.

When David was an old, grey-haired man he was a very wise man. He even prayed that God would not let him die until he had told the next generation about God's love! Wow, from a young boy to an old man God chose him and used him in lots of different ways!

He was a real Bible hero.

Round-up

With all the different seasons comes plenty of variety. Spring reminds us of new life – young people full of life and energy. Summer reminds us of strength, the strength that comes with 'middle aged' people, often well established with plenty of ideas. Autumn and winter remind us of trees that have been around a long time, like older people who have plenty of experience and wisdom.

In the Bible, God chose many different people to do different things. Sometimes he chose children, or young people, because of their excitement, energy and strength. Other times he chose older people because of their experience and wisdom. Let's enjoy the variety of the seasons and also the different age groups of people. Let's show respect for one another and enjoy each other's company, like God does.

Prayer

Thank you, Father, for older people with their wisdom and experience. Thank you also for young people with their energy and excitement. We thank you that we can do so much when we all work together.
Amen.

Be fair

to books

 Aim

To show the importance of books. Showing how books can be fun and exciting to read, but also how we can learn so much from them. Another aim is to show why the Bible is such an important book to Christians.

Song

Image of God (*Come On, Let's Celebrate*)

 Puppet sketch

(*Micky refuses to come out of his bag*)

John   Come on, Micky! We're meant to take this assembly!

Micky   I'm reading!

John   I'm pleased to hear that, but can't you put it down for a second?

Micky   No! It's too exciting!

John   Come on out. You can bring the book.

Micky   (*Micky comes out with the book in his mouth*) Hold this, please. (*He gives John the book to hold and carries on reading – mime laughing and shaking. John tries to talk to him, but Micky is too engrossed in his book*)

John   (*To the audience*) I think we'd better leave him to it . . . (*he puts Micky back in the bag. Micky carries on reading*) As you can see, books can be so gripping – you just can't put them down.

Illustration

I've brought along four of my books for you to see.

- *A book that teaches:* Produce a book that teaches you something. It may be a book on juggling, magic tricks, cooking, a sport or a hobby. Demonstrate what it has taught you. Books can teach you how to do lots of exciting things.
- *A Highway Code:* Ask the children if they know what this book is for. Draw out some of the road signs and see if they can tell you what they mean. This book is full of rules and regulations to help me stay safe when I'm using the roads.
- *A novel:* Outline the plot of the story. Story books can be so exciting and full of adventures. Sometimes it's so hard to put the book down, a bit like Micky and his book.
- *The Bible:* To Christians this is the most important book of all. It's God's book to us. It teaches lots of important things. It's full of

instructions to help us live on Earth. It's full of exciting stories about kings and queens, giants and battles, Jesus and God's love for us.

Bible story

This story from the Bible is called 'The Lost Book' and can be found in 2 Kings 22 and 2 Chronicles 34:14-33.

'The King is dead!' it was announced. 'Good!' cried the people, because the king had been evil, selfish, and greedy – and cruel to his own people.

'But who will rule us now?' said one of the old king's advisers. 'The king's son is only 8 years old – he's just a boy!'

Maybe one of the advisers said something like this. 'Yes, he's 8 years old, isn't that good news! We'll be able to get him to do whatever we like! We'll be as powerful as the king himself.'

So the boy Josiah was made the new king at the age of 8 years old! But even so, King Josiah was no fool, and he wasn't going to be bossed around by anyone. He had his own ideas. He called his advisers together and said: 'Look, we are meant to be God's chosen people, but look at his temple – it's in ruins, it's disgraceful! There is nowhere for God's people to worship their God! Set to work on rebuilding God's temple straight away!'

They were all amazed to hear him speaking with such authority and wisdom, and they obeyed what he said and started rebuilding the temple immediately! While they were clearing away some of the rubbish, a man found a very old book, so he took it to the boy king.

'Your Majesty, I have found a book! What do you want me to do with it?'

'May I have a look?' said King Josiah.

He started to read it and as he did his eyes lit up with delight.

'Quick, stop all the work and gather the people!' said the king.

'What . . . everyone?' came the reply.

'Yes, everyone. I don't want anyone to miss out,' said the king.

The people all gathered together and sat down to listen to the king as he read from this very old book. You could have heard a pin drop as the king read the pages. The people were all amazed by what they heard. It was all about how God wanted them to live in his wonderful world. The king went on reading for hour after hour, but still they listened!

When he finally finished, all the people were so moved by what they had heard that they all made a promise that they would try to live in God's world the way that he wanted them to live – the lost book had changed their lives!

Round-up

Books can be great fun. They teach us lots of things to do, or they are full of good advice, or they are exciting stories. So be fair to books.

Prayer

Lord, thank you for books and all that they teach us. Thank you for your book, the Bible, and all that it teaches us.
Amen.

Be kind to one another!

Aim
To show that if someone is mean to you it's easy to be mean back to them! But if we can show kindness instead, then sometimes a nasty situation can change into a great time!

Songs
Be kind and compassionate (*Bible Explosion*)
Jesus went out of his way (*Bible Explosion*)
Never, never, never (*Come On, Let's Celebrate*)

Puppet sketch

John	Hey, Micky! (*Sniff!*) You often smell like you've just had a banana but I know you love them so you normally *have* just had one! But today it smells like you've had a whole bunch of bananas!
Micky	I have!
John	How come?
Micky	You know Bad Billy Baboon!
John	Oh yeah, what's he been up to now?
Micky	The other day my mum gave me the biggest banana I'd ever seen. Well, I must admit I was showing off with it, holding it up high so everyone could see it when suddenly Bad Billy Baboon dashed out from nowhere and ran off with it!
John	Oh dear!
Micky	He wasn't getting away with that! No way! I took up the chase! But he'd already peeled it and shoved it in his mouth – whole! Then he threw the skin over his head. Guess what happened next?
John	I dread to think!
Micky	I slipped on the banana skin and slid over, falling in some mud!
John	Not a pretty sight!
Micky	I was so upset, but everyone was on my side and told me they would help me sort him out!
John	I don't like the sound of that!
Micky	Next morning, I couldn't believe my eyes. The banana Mum gave me was even bigger than the day before! I was so happy I forgot what had happened and once again I was showing it off! When suddenly, guess what happened?

John	Bad Billy Baboon dashed out and stole your banana!
Micky	Wow, how did you know that? But it's true! Just like the day before he ran off with my banana! I took up the chase, but he wasn't looking where he was going. He was trying to run and peel the banana all at the same time. He slipped on some mud and went flying. He ended up with banana all over his face, and the banana skin on his head and mud all over his clothes!
John	Gosh!
Micky	Everyone roared with laughter. He looked so funny! Everyone shouted out: 'Serves you right!' Which it did! But then some of the guys became really nasty and started throwing stones at him! They told me to kick him while he was down.
John	This is turning really nasty!
Micky	I could see Bad Billy Baboon was really hurt. This was my big chance!
John	What?
Micky	I went over to him!
John	(*Looking worried*) And?
Micky	Helped him up and took him off to the first-aid room. Everyone thought I was going to hit him, but what would that have achieved!
John	Good for you.
Micky	Big Bad Billy Baboon came up to me today! And to my amazement he said sorry, and thanked me for helping him, and gave me a huge bunch of bananas! So now we're friends for life!
John	Great to hear it! Let's go!
Micky	Bye everyone!

Bible story

2 Kings 6:8-23

There were two kings in the Bible who hated one another, the king of Aram and the king of Israel. The king of Aram had a great idea. He said to his men: 'Men, we are going to such and such a place, where we'll hide, and when the king of Israel comes here with his army we'll ambush them, jump out and attack them. They won't be ready for battle so we're bound to win!'

'Cor! What a great plan,' thought his men.

But Elisha, a great man of God, said to the king of Israel: 'Don't go to such and such a place today, because the king of Aram is there with his men, ready to attack you! So the king of Aram waited . . . and waited . . . and waited . . . but the king of Israel never showed up!

'Oh blow,' said the king. 'What a waste of a day!' Tomorrow we'll go to such and such a road . . . they always go along there!'

But guess what happened. The great man of God, Elisha, warned the king of Israel again! And it happened again the next day, and the next day, and the next day . . . until finally the king of Aram shouted at his men: 'Who is telling the king of Israel where we will be! Who is the traitor?'

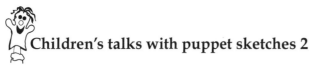

'Err, it's none of us, King, it's Elisha, the man of God,' said one of the men! The king of Aram was furious!

'Send an army to his house and sort him out!' demanded the king. Next morning Elisha's servant opened the curtains and looked outside.

'What a beautiful morning! The sun is in the sky, the birds are singing in the trees, and we are surrounded by lots of horrible soldiers!' Aghhh! Panic! 'Elisha!' he shouted. 'We're surrounded by soldiers!'

'Don't panic,' said Elisha and then he prayed to God: 'Open my servant's eyes.'

The servant probably thought: 'I have got my eyes open!' but as he was looking, suddenly he saw the Lord's army on the hills ready to protect them! 'Wow!' he thought. Then Elisha prayed again, saying: 'Close the eyes of the king of Aram's soldiers.' Suddenly none of the soldiers could see!

Elisha went out to them and said: 'You look a bit lost, guys. Let me lead you!' But he led them to the city of Samaria, where the king of Israel and his army lived! The king of Israel couldn't believe his eyes. Here was Elisha leading the king of Aram's army into his city, and they were blind. They pointed their spears and arrows at them!

Then the Lord opened the eyes of the soldiers and when they saw where they were they were terrified!

'What shall I do with them?' shouted the king of Israel. 'Shall I kill them?!'

'No!' said Elisha. 'Give them a drink of water. They look thirsty and hungry – prepare a feast for them, and let's have a party!'

The army of Aram couldn't believe their ears. They had a wonderful feast and made lots of new friends and they went back to the king of Aram and told him what a wonderful bunch the Israelites were, and how they had been so kind to them! And guess what? There were no more battles or fighting for many, many years. The people enjoyed living in peace together!

Round-up

Wouldn't it be wonderful if we could all learn the lesson from this story and learn to forgive each other and not to retaliate, but to be kind to each other instead! How wonderful the school, the town, the country and the world would be if we all learnt to live like this.

Prayer

Lord, thank you for this wonderful story. Please help us to learn the lesson from it and be kind and compassionate to one another.
Amen.

Big-head!

 Aim
Some people don't realise that they are special and important. But some people think that they're the greatest, and that they're much better than everyone else!

Songs
Nobody's a nobody (*Come On, Let's Celebrate*)
Hope in the Lord (*Bible Explosion*)

 Puppet sketch

Micky	One of my mates is like I used to be. Very shy!
John	You! Very shy?!
Micky	Very quiet!
John	You! Very quiet!!
Micky	No confidence!
John	You! With no confidence?
Micky	I said used to be!
John	I was going to say!
Micky	So I told him . . .
John	(*Interrupting*) Who?
Micky	My friend who is very shy and quiet with no confidence!
John	Oh yeah!
Micky	So I told him that he is special and unique, and that there is no one in the whole wide world like him! There never has been and never will be! So he's got plenty to offer – so don't be shy!
John	Wow! That sounds excellent!
Micky	But I also thought I ought to point out that although he is unique and special he's still got a long way to go before he catches me up!
John	(*In disbelief of what he has just heard*) Pardon! What do you mean by that?
Micky	Well, he'll never be as fast as me! Never be as good looking as me, or a babe magnet like me . . .
John	(*A little bit annoyed*) Possibly, but he'll develop other gifts and skills!
Micky	(*Not really listening*) . . . Or be as clever as me or be able to play football like

me, or be as good on the PlayStation as me or (*getting more and more carried away!!*) be able to climb trees as quickly as me or be as good at singing as me or . . .

John	(*Interrupting*) Have such a big head as me!
Micky	(*Copying John, without realising what he is about to say*) . . . or have such a big head as me. (*Micky suddenly realises what he has said*) A big head? I haven't got a big head!
John	You should have heard yourself then.
Micky	But I am good at all of those things!
John	Your friend is shy and has no confidence, but it's far worse to have a big head and be overconfident. You'll soon have no friends if you keep telling them that they aren't as good as you are. That reminds me of a story in the Bible.

Bible story

Daniel 4 – The king's dream

There was once a powerful, mighty king called Nebuchadnezzar. His kingdom was huge – just like his name!

One night he had a dream about a tree in the middle of the earth. It grew bigger and bigger until it reached the sky and could be seen by everyone in the whole world! The tree grew bigger and it had beautiful leaves and was loaded down with wonderful fruit. Wild animals rested in the shade and ate the fruit, and birds built nests in its branches!

Suddenly, an angel appeared and in a loud voice shouted: 'Cut down the tree, drive the animals and birds away and leave the stump where it is for the grass to grow over it.' Then the angel looked at the king and said: 'Drive him out and let him live with the animals and plants!'

This dream obviously upset the great, powerful King Nebuchadnezzar, and so he called for his royal advisers and asked them to tell him what the dream meant. But none of them knew, so then he called for Daniel. Daniel was a godly, wise man but when he heard the dream he was most upset.

'The tree in the dream is like you and your kingdom, oh king!' said Daniel. 'Mighty and powerful – in fact the most mighty and powerful kingdom in the whole world – but God is more powerful and if you forget this, then God will drive you out of your kingdom and you will live with the animals and plants.'

'Gosh, thanks for the warning,' the king replied.

Many years later when King Nebuchadnezzar had forgotten all about the dream he looked over his kingdom and he was so proud and said: 'Look how great Babylon is. I built it as my capital city to display my power, my might, my glory and my majesty.

'How great, how fantastic, how wonderful I am! There is no king as great as me!'

As he was saying this he suddenly became like an animal running out of the palace and into the forest. He lived like a wild animal, eating grass. His hair grew like an eagle's feathers and his nails like claws! Daniel had warned him not to be a proud, big-headed king, otherwise the dream would become true – and that was what had happened.

Seven years passed, when one night the king looked up into the sky. He saw the moon and the wonderful stars that filled the whole sky, and he fell on his knees and praised the Lord. He realised that God's kingdom was far greater than his, and that God was more powerful, more wonderful, and more glorious than any earthly king.

As soon as he honoured God, he became well again and he went back to being a great king in a great kingdom, but now he realised that it was God who had given him all this, so it was God who was truly great!

Round-up   If you're really good at something then don't become a big-head and a show-off! We need to realise that we are all special and we all have different talents. Work hard and do your best to develop your talent and then use it to entertain or help others!

Prayer   Father God, thank you for all the gifts you give us! Help us not to show them off but to use them wisely. Thank you that you are so great, but you do so much for us.
Amen.

Couldn't get through

 Aim   A theme on prayer. Even though God is so great and powerful, he thinks of us as his children and wants us to talk to him like we would talk to a good father who has time for us and is interested in what we say!

Songs   Pray, pray (*Bible Explosion*)
A huge thank you (*Come On, Let's Celebrate*)

Puppet sketch

Micky	(*To John*) I don't suppose you have time to listen either.
John	Of course I have . . . what's up!
Micky	You have! Really?
John	Yeah!
Micky	Yeah, but I don't suppose you're really interested though, are you?
John	Of course I am, Micky. You're my mate!
Micky	Oh wow, I've got some great news! I've been invited along to an audition to sing in a new pop group, similar to Pop Idol!
John	Wow! Micky, that's really exciting! I'm surprised you seem so down about it! What's up?
Micky	Well, it's such great news I had to tell someone so I thought about who I could phone to tell the good news. 'I know,' I thought, 'I'll tell Britney Spears. I love her music so she's bound to be interested to know I am going to be a pop star like her!'
John	Wow, you phoned Britney Spears! What did she say?
Micky	Nothing! I tried and tried and tried to find her telephone number but couldn't! I went on-line to send an e-mail but she never replied!
John	Shame, but I'm not surprised . . . she must have thousands of people trying to speak to her every day, so she couldn't possibly speak to them all!
Micky	Yeah, I suppose you're right. So then I tried to tell Mum, but she was on the phone to someone. In fact she's probably still on the phone!
John	Knowing your mum, you're probably right!
Micky	So then I tried to tell Dad but he was cutting the lawn and it was hard to make myself heard. He was nodding away but I could tell he wasn't listening.

	I could have said anything and he'd still have been nodding away!
John	Well, yes it's hard to have a conversation and cut the grass at the same time!
Micky	Then I tried to tell my brother, but he was playing a computer game at the time and once again he wasn't interested! You're the first person I've managed to tell.
John	What was that? Sorry, I wasn't listening!
Micky	What!!!!!
John	Only joking! It's great news! Well done, Micky.

Bible story

Luke 18:9-14 – Jesus told this story

Two men come into the temple to pray. The first one walks down the aisle, picks a spot right at the front and stands up straight. He lifts his head up, lifts his hands up, and clears his throat. Is he ready? Is he steady? Yep! He's off!!!! 'Dear God . . . thank you for making me the way I am!'

He prayed in a very loud voice to make sure that God and everyone else could hear him!

'You have noticed, no doubt, that I am a regular temple attender, here every Sabbath . . . on the dot, always prompt and punctual. I live a good, holy, religious life, not like some of those who pop off to the pub after evening prayers. I have a steady job and work hard for a living, unlike some of those who think 'signing on' once a fortnight is enough of an effort!

'Yes, steady job and steady wife, I don't eye up other ladies or commit, er, (*whispers*) adultery (*glances around and continues*). I put 10 per cent in the collection every week and on top of that . . . as an extra bonus . . . !!! (*He stops for a breath, then speaks even louder to make doubly sure that God hears him*)

'. . . I sent £20 to 'Comic Relief'. (*Round of applause from others*) I do all the right things and I don't do all the wrong things. I don't swear, or at least not out loud, I don't steal and I don't even fiddle my tax returns. I don't tell lies, I don't listen to bad jokes and I'm kind to my neighbours!

'All in all, I'd say I'm the kind of person you want people to be. I bet you wish the rest were like me!

'Thank you, oh thank you, dear God, that I am the way I am. Thank you so much that I'm not like that other person over there!

'Well, in the name of the Father, the Son and the Holy Ghost . . . whoops, wrong! I mean in the name of our great father Abraham, Isaac and Jacob, *Amen*!'

With this, our friend gathers up all his scriptures under his arm and walks boldly down the centre of the temple. He pauses to shake hands with the steward, calls his wife to hurry up and goes home, feeling smug, self-righteous, but as empty as empty can be. He's done it all before, week in, week out, and he'll continue for many years to come!

But here comes another man to pray, sneaking in through the door, giving

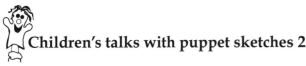

nervous glances over his shoulder as he kneels on the floor behind the back pew. He says nothing for a few moments, and he seems pretty speechless. Hang on, he's saying something!

'Mutter, mutter, mutter. (*Whisper*) God, have mercy on me, a sinner!' But no one heard a word of it! Why do people mumble like that? He's got up and walked out as sneakily as he came in – a bit dodgy if you ask me, and what a non event!

But the second person who prayed had spoken to God. He just said: 'Be good to me God, because I'm a bad man,' and God heard him! And God has forgiven him. As the second person went home he didn't look any different or have a halo, but he'd just spoken to God – and he felt brand new!!!

Round-up

God is far greater than any celebrity, star or politician. After all, he is the creator of all things, including all so-called celebrities. But it's clear from the Bible that God is interested in us. He thinks of us as his children! When Jesus spoke about prayer with his disciples he said: 'Pray like this – "Our Father, who is in Heaven."'

So think of God as a good, kind and loving father who has time for his children. You can pray about anything, but often people say: 'Why should God be interested in me, and in any case, I wouldn't know what to say.'

And some people think God is like Father Christmas and they only pray when they want something.

Illustration

When my boy was 2 years old he started to learn to talk. When he talked he didn't have a speech prepared and what he said didn't make a lot of sense, but I loved to hear him talk to me. Of course, I still do – and he makes a lot more sense!

Prayer

Dear Heavenly Father, thank you that although you are so great and powerful you have time for us. Thank you that you want us to talk to you, like a loving parent loves to hear their children talk.
Amen.

Don't forget
to remember

Ideal date  **Aim**	Remembrance Week To show how important it is to remember certain things. Especially when someone has done something special for you. It's important not to forget.
Songs	Anytime, anywhere (*Come On, Let's Celebrate*) V.I.P. (*Come On, Let's Celebrate*)
Puppet sketch	
Introduction	(*To the children*) When I went to blow my nose this morning I discovered my hanky had a knot in it. Can anyone tell me why that might be? Yes, I need to remember something really important, but to be honest I can't remember what I am meant to remember!
John	I can't even remember putting a knot in my hanky! I wonder if Micky knows anything about it. Micky, I have a knot in my hanky. Do you know why?
Micky	Yes, to help you remember.
John	Remember what?
Micky	Oh, no! You haven't forgotten what you're meant to remember, have you?
John	Yes, in fact I can't even remember putting the knot in my hanky in the first place!
Micky	You didn't! I put the knot in your hanky, not you! I did it to help you remember what you're meant not to forget! But you've forgotten! (*Micky raises his eyebrows in disgust*)
John	No wonder I can't remember, if you put the knot in my hanky!
Micky	It's such an important day you shouldn't need a knot to remember. (*Looks up again, and tuts*)
John	(*Whispers to children*) He thinks I've forgotten, but I haven't really. Happy Birthday, Micky! (*Micky looks up and excitedly bops around. John slips a birthday card in his mouth*) I think he's speechless. We had better let him go and open his card!
Illustration	We forget things so easily! Kim's Game – Have 15 objects on a tray. Show the children each object one

at a time. Cover them with a cloth. Ask the children to put up their hands if they can remember an object. See if they can remember all 15!

Did you notice how upset Micky was when he thought I had forgotten his birthday? But then you saw how happy he was when he knew I had remembered! It's so important not to forget to remember, but we all forget so easily. So we need things to help us remember.

Bible story

In the Bible a group of people called the Israelites had been slaves in Egypt for many years. God did some amazing things and eventually they were set free. They were so happy to be free but they soon started grumbling and moaning.

'Here, Moses, give us some water, give us more food, take us back to Egypt!' the people cried!

What? Had they forgotten what it was like to be slaves, being beaten for no reason! Had they forgotten that God had rescued them in such an amazing way!

The next generation did reach the promised land and enjoyed all the freedom that brought. But to help them remember how terrible it was to be slaves and how God had rescued them, they now have a special feast, a time of celebration and remembrance called 'The Passover Festival'.
(*Ask the children*)

- What do Christians remember at Christmas?
- What do Christians remember at Easter?
- Diaries and photographs help us to remember. I am wearing something very important – a poppy!

Round-up

Many older people can remember the war. They remember friends and family who were killed in the war. Many older people are slow at walking and may slow us down from time to time, but remember when they were younger they did something really great for us! They risked their lives so that we can be free. Many others gave their lives so that we can be free. So we need to remember what a great thing they did for us!

Prayer

Lord, help us to remember the important things that happen in our lives and also help us to remember to thank people who do things for us.
Amen.

Don't worry –
be happy!

Aim Christians believe that God is in control. Christians also believe that Jesus had the same power and God wants us to trust in him.

Songs Trust in the Lord (*Come On, Let's Celebrate*)
Do you not know (*Come On, Let's Celebrate*)
Hope in the Lord (*Bible Explosion*)

Puppet sketch

John	Micky, how did you get on? (*To audience*) Micky went to work with his dad yesterday. His dad is a master plasterer. Was it fun?
Micky	Fun! No way! It was hard work and I got covered in plaster. That bit was fun!
John	(*To audience*) Just in case you don't know what a plasterer is . . .
Micky	(*Interrupting*) I always thought he put plasters on people who had cut themselves so when he told me that he put plaster on walls I was very confused. I pictured a wall covered in sticky plasters, very funny, but why? That's why he took me to work to show me!
John	When a builder builds a wall inside a building it's normally made out of grey blocks, which are not very nice to look at and are a bit rough. So a plasterer covers the wall with what is called plaster. It makes the wall smooth! Then a painter paints the wall.
Micky	He let me have a go. Plaster is all sloppy when you put it on, then you have to make it smooth and then it dries on the wall! But I dropped more plaster on the floor than on the wall! It was a right mess so he showed me how to hold the plasterer's trowel and how to put it on the wall. It was very messy but great fun!
John	Excellent!
Micky	Then I turned round to ask Dad something but he had gone! I panicked! 'Dad, Dad,' I shouted!
John	Why?
Micky	I'd put all the plaster on the wall but it wasn't smooth, in fact it was lumpy. I tried to smooth it out but the more I tried the worse it became. It was too thick here, too thin there. I made grooves and holes all over the plaster!

John	Oh dear!
Micky	It was drying quickly! It would be a real mess if it dried like that! Oh where was he? 'Help, Dad!' Why didn't he come?
John	Maybe he's . . .
Micky	(*Interrupting*) Finally I gave up on him. He had let me down! I was tired after all that work and nodded off to sleep. I had a nightmare about the people who bought the house trying to paper the walls but it was like trying to paper over a mountain range. Finally I woke up! Wow, I thought!
John	What?
Micky	Amazing!
John	What's amazing!
Mickyv	The wall!
John	Oh dear, don't tell me. Which mountain range was it like?
Micky	The plaster was as smooth as a baby's bottom!
John	As smooth as a baby's bottom? We don't want to know! Actually we do! How did that happen?
Micky	My dad had sorted it! Apparently, when you plaster you put the plaster on the wall but you don't try and make it perfectly smooth straight away. You leave it for a bit and let it begin to dry and then just at the right moment you smooth it out. My dad had just popped to the toilet. When he got back I was fast asleep and he didn't want to wake me up.
John	So he hadn't let you down after all. He knew exactly what he was doing and you could trust him.
Micky	Yep, he's a brilliant plasterer. Thanks to him many people have got smooth walls in their living rooms!

Bible story

Luke 8:22-25 - Calming of the storm

After a really busy day it's good to relax. Jesus and his disciples had had a busy day so they jumped on Simon Peter's boat and headed off onto the lake. It was a pleasant evening and the water was calm. Some of the disciples may have done a spot of fishing while others may have just chatted and joked together.

But after a while the wind started to blow, which meant that the water became rough and the boat started to rock. 'Oh dear,' said those who weren't used to the rough waters, 'we're feeling a little ill!' But the wind carried on getting stronger and stronger, which meant the waves were getting higher and higher and the boat was being tossed around even more. 'Oh dear' said the fishermen, 'we're feeling scared!' This was bad news! When the fishermen admit to being scared, then they must be in great danger! One of them shouted over the noise of the storm: 'Where is Jesus?' When they saw him they couldn't believe their eyes – there he was sleeping peacefully while the storm raged around them! They grabbed him and woke him up and shouted,

'Don't you care that we are going to die?' Jesus calmly stood up in the boat and in a gentle voice said, 'Peace!' Wow, they couldn't believe it! There was peace. The wind stopped blowing, the water was calm and the boat sat gently in the water! Jesus said to the disciples: 'Where is your faith?' But for once the disciples were speechless. Then they looked at one another and said, 'Who is this man that even the wind and the waves obey him?'

Round-up

The disciples would have been taught as children that it was only God who had power over the sea and the sky and yet here was Jesus with the same power! Christians believe that God is in ultimate control so there's no need to worry. Christians also believe that God the creator became a man and this is who Jesus is!

Prayer

Thank you, God, that you are so powerful but you are also kind and have time for us. So we don't need to worry.
Amen.

Excuses, excuses

 Aim

To show that sometimes we miss out on something amazing – and it's all because we can't be bothered to have a go!

Songs

For God so loved the world (*Come On, Let's Celebrate*)
Thank you, mate (*Come On, Let's Celebrate*)

 Puppet sketch

John	Shame you couldn't come, but did you have a good day building that tree house?
Micky	No, it rained all day.
John	Did it? Gosh we had sunshine!
Micky	Oh yeah, you went to your grandad's, didn't you?
John	Yes! But not just me – Barry, Ralph, Gordon and Shaz were there, too. You should have come!
Micky	Ha! I don't think so. I bet you all watched a gardening programme on TV! Followed by stories about what school was like when your grandad was young. He probably read to you from a book with long, hard words that sent you all to sleep!
John	You're so wrong, Micky! He did tell some stories about when he was young but they . . . (*Micky interrupts*)
Micky	(*Interrupting*) See! Told you!
John	. . . were great – really interesting. When we first arrived, he showed us some tricks, then after that we played games! You would have loved it! Then he took us to McDonald's for lunch – a Big Mac and fries followed by chocolate ice cream . . .
Micky	Oh, what! My favourite!
John	Then he took us in the car.
Micky	(*Sarcastically*) Great!
John	. . . to the seaside! We played on the beach and went to the fair!
Micky	What?!?
John	You missed an excellent day!
Micky	OK, don't keep going on about it. To be honest, I thought visiting your grandad sounded a bit boring but it sounds like you had a great time!

John	We did! You really missed out on a great day!
Micky	Can I come next time?
John	Of course.
Micky	I'll go and get ready – bye!

Bible story

Luke 14:15-24 – This is a parable (a story with a meaning) told by Jesus

A certain man was preparing a great feast, a banquet! In those days people didn't have holidays, so from time to time nice rich people or kings would put on special banquets for their friends and the people who worked for them.

There would have been dancing, games and – of course – loads of yummy food! It was a lot of hard work to organise, and expensive, but it was all worth it in the end.

At last this banquet was ready, so the rich man sent his servants out to tell those he had invited. The servant knocked on the first door and said: 'You received an invitation to the master's feast. Now everything is ready, so come and enjoy the banquet!'

'I can't come,' came the response. 'I've just bought a field and I haven't seen it yet.'

The servant must have been astonished, because he said: 'What? Well why don't you go and see the field after the banquet – after all, the field won't be going anywhere!'

'I can't do that,' came the reply and the man slammed the door in the servant's face!

The servant tried the next door. 'You received an invitation to the master's feast. Now come, for everything is ready – come and enjoy the banquet!'

'I can't come,' came the reply. 'I've just bought some oxen – they're like big cows, just in case you don't know. They'll pull my plough and I haven't seen them yet!'

'You mean to say that you've bought some oxen and you haven't seen them yet!' said the surprised servant. 'That's daft. They may be all skinny and weak. Come along to the banquet, it's going to be great!'

'No thanks,' came the cross reply, and he also slammed the door in the servant's face.

The servant must have been amazed by the two responses. Finally, he knocked on the last door and said to the young couple standing there: 'You received an invitation to the master's feast. Now come, for everything is ready. Come and enjoy the banquet!'

'We can't come!' they said. 'We've just got married! Kissy-kissy.'

'All the more reason to come!' said the servant. 'You can have a great time dancing and dining together at the banquet!'

But once more the response came back: 'No thanks!' And they, too, slammed the door in his face.

The servant went back with the bad news that none of those who the master had invited were coming. But the master was determined that his feast should not go to waste. He wanted to see his house full of people enjoying themselves, so he told his servants to go into the streets and invite the homeless to his party. Of course, they didn't make any excuses and they had a wonderful time!

Round-up

It says in the Bible that God has invited us all to follow him and to be a part of his family. He tells us that one day we'll be with him in heaven, and it will be a bit like a banquet. But lots of people choose not to accept the invitation and make up all sorts of excuses. Christians say that those who choose not to follow him are missing out on the most important and wonderful invitation anyone can ever receive!

Prayer

Thank you, heavenly Father, that you have gone to all this trouble to organise a fantastic banquet for us. Help us to be grateful and to accept your invitation. *Amen.*

Fair and square

Aim To help children to see why we need rules and why we need to obey them.

Songs Image of God (*Come On, Let's Celebrate*)
Think about such things (*Come On, Let's Celebrate*)

Puppet sketch

(Micky comes out with a bandage round his arm)

John	Oh, Micky! What have you done?
Micky	I've hurt my arm and I want some symphony!
John	You mean sympathy! What happened?
Micky	I went up the park with some friends to play football. Some guys came along and challenged us to a match.
John	So you did this playing football?
Micky	Sort of . . . the other guys said that we would play without any rules – everyone could do as they liked!
John	What? You can't play football without any rules!
Micky	We know that now, but at the time it sounded like a great idea! No rules, do as you like, no one to tell you what you can and can't do. No one blowing the whistle and stopping the game all the time!
John	Oh, dear. What happened?
Micky	One minute they had ten goalies, then they ran off with the goal posts! They picked up the ball when they weren't meant to, but were allowed to because there weren't any rules!
John	Oh, dear. It doesn't sound like much fun to me.
Micky	The one time I had the ball, I dribbled it past the first player, passed to the next and the next. Then suddenly they all jumped on me and picked up the ball and ran off with it! That's when I hurt my arm!
John	So was it a good game?
Micky	No! It was stupid! It wasn't a game at all! It was a riot and they stole the ball!
John	So do you prefer football with rules, or without them?
Micky	With them! Football needs rules so everyone knows what they are allowed to do and are not to do. Then you can have a really good game. Fair and square!

Illustration

Draw these signs from the Highway Code:

- A 40 mph speed limit
- A 'No Entry' sign
- Traffic lights

Show a Highway Code book and ask the question: 'What is this?'

Then show the signs and ask what they mean.

All these signs are there to help us keep safe and they must be obeyed! If there were no road signs the road would be a very dangerous place. There would be lots of accidents.

Bible story

Exodus 20:1-17 – The Ten Commandments

The children of Israel had been slaves for hundreds of years. This meant that they had to work hard for no reward, and if they didn't work hard enough they would be beaten. They had no freedom.

Then God sent Moses, and after quite a time the Israelites were set free! Free at last! No one to tell them what to do! But the people soon started to fight and steal. Moses went up a mountain called Mount Sinai and the Lord spoke to him and gave him the Ten Commandments.

Here are a few:

- Remember the Sabbath and keep it holy! The Sabbath was a special day for the Jews, similar to our Sunday. God told the people: 'Don't work every day, but have a day off, spend time with your family and spend time with me.'
- Respect your parents: Your parents do lots for you, like providing meals and clothes and a home. They love you and want you to love them back and not take them for granted.
- Do not steal! I bet you get upset if someone steals something that is precious to you! So don't steal from one another – it just causes fights and ill feelings.

There are lots more. But remember, if God made the world then he must know the best way to live in it – so follow his instructions.

Round-up

Rules are important. If there are no rules then it is dangerous with people doing what they want to do. When one person disobeys a rule then someone always gets hurt.

Prayer

Lord, thank you for your rules – the Ten Commandments. Help us to realise how important it is to follow them.
Amen.

Heaven is a wonderful place

 Aim

Christians believe that when they die they will go to be with Jesus in heaven, but what does the Bible say heaven is like and how do you get there?

Song

Hope in the Lord (*Bible Explosion*)

 Puppet sketch

John	Micky, I heard you went camping the other night! How did you get on?
Micky	After I put the tent up I turned round to fetch the pegs, then when I turned back to it the tent had fallen down! I had to start all over again.
John	Oh dear! Did you get the tent up in the end?
Micky	Oh yes, but then as I was going off to sleep I felt something walking across my face. Eight little legs with little feet – a spider!
John	Did it put you off?
Micky	No, of course not! It was good fun. I had a nice sleep snuggled up in my sleeping bag.
John	Good!
Micky	Then I woke up and thought: 'Isn't it wonderful looking at the beautiful clear sky.' I could see the moon and the stars. Then I saw a shooting star. Wow it was beautiful. That's when I realised there was something missing! The tent!
John	Oh dear!
Micky	So I gave up and went in the house!
John	In the house?
Micky	Yeah! Well it was my first time. I didn't want to do anything too adventurous. Camping was fun but I prefer my home with my nice, warm bedroom and my soft bed any day!

Bible story

Luke 18:18-23 – The rich man

One day a very rich young man came to Jesus and asked: 'Good teacher, what must I do to receive eternal life?'

   What a strange question to ask. Maybe he knew that he had everything he wanted – after all he was very rich. He probably had a very nice house, a big, posh chariot with fast, strong horses. He may have even had a swimming pool! He certainly would have had servants! Anything he ever wanted he just went out and bought!

But there was one thing he knew he couldn't buy anywhere and that was eternal life – he wanted to book a place in heaven.

Jesus replied: 'You know the commandments – don't murder, don't steal, respect your father and mother.'

'Great,' said the rich young man. 'Ever since I was a child I have kept these.'

But Jesus went on to say: 'Sell all that you have, give your money to the poor and come and follow me, then you will have riches in heaven!'

The rich young man's face dropped. He didn't want to sell everything and give his money to the poor – so he went away sad. But Jesus had promised him riches in heaven.

Jesus didn't mean that we have to sell everything in order to go to heaven – he just wants us to realise that there is nothing on earth that can compare to the riches of heaven.

Round-up

Christians believe that if you choose to follow Jesus, when you die you will go to be with him in heaven. But what is heaven like?

The Bible describes our life on earth as being like living in a tent. Camping can be loads of fun, but what if the tent leaks or blows down in a really bad storm? Often during our lives we will have things go wrong, there will be sadness and hard times. A house is far more secure and less likely to leak or be blown away. That's what the Bible says heaven is like – it's like being in a secure room and a welcoming home! There will be no more sad times, and it will be a place of rejoicing and happiness.

Prayer

Father, thank you for all the things we have that are so precious. Thank you that you promise to those who follow you a home in heaven that is more wonderful than anything we can ever imagine.
Amen.

I don't
believe it!

Aim

To show that the Easter story of Jesus rising from the dead is such an amazing story that people struggle to believe it. But the story is the heart of the Christian message. Millions of people right down the ages do believe this story and they believe Jesus is still alive and has changed their lives.

Songs

For God so loved the world (*Come On, Let's Celebrate*)
On Good Friday (*Come On, Let's Celebrate*)

Puppet sketch

Micky	John, you'll never guess what I saw yesterday on the way to school!
John	No, you're probably right.
Micky	I saw an elephant! A whopping great elephant!
John	(*Bursts out laughing, thinking Micky is joking*) You're pulling my leg!
Micky	(*Looks confused*) I'm nowhere near your leg!
John	So you saw an elephant, did you? Big deal! I saw a giraffe riding a bicycle, and a lion being taken for a walk, and a monkey driving a bus!
Micky	Did you?
John	No! But you didn't really see an elephant did you!
Micky	Yes!
John	What . . . was he playing on the swings?
Micky	Don't be silly, he would break them!
John	Playing football?
Micky	(*A little sad*) You don't believe me do you?
John	Now, if we lived in Africa or in India I probably would believe you, but I don't think elephants have ever roamed freely round England.
Micky	But, but . . .
John	Now if you said you'd seen a fox, a squirrel or even a deer I might believe you . . . but an elephant?
Micky	Don't you trust me?
John	Yes, of course but . . .
Micky	(*Micky is cross and produces a newspaper clipping*) Read this!
John	(*Reads the headline*) 'Elephant escapes from travelling circus!' Gosh, it's true!

Micky	See!
John	I'm sorry I doubted you, Micky.

Bible story

John 20:24-29 – Doubting Thomas

Have you ever missed something really special? Something that everyone else saw, but you missed because you weren't there!

This happened to a guy in the Bible. He had been with his best friends in a room together. Normally when they were all together they had a great time, with plenty of jokes, fun and sharing stories, but it wasn't like that any more. Now when they met together they cried and they were scared. Their best friend, Jesus, had been taken away by the Romans and they had put him to death on a cross. It was the end of something very special and they didn't know what to do now.

One of them – a guy called Thomas – decided to go out, but when he came back the atmosphere in the room had completely changed. All the rest of them were laughing and smiling just like they used to when Jesus was alive.

'What's going on?' Thomas said.

'He's been here with us,' they said.

'Who has?' he said.

'Who do you think? Jesus has!' they replied.

'Don't be daft! Jesus is dead! You're all going mad. Go out and get some fresh air.'

'It's true, Thomas. You have to believe us,' they all said.

'Unless I see the scars on his hands and his side I will not believe,' Thomas replied. Suddenly the room went quiet and Thomas couldn't believe his eyes. Standing in front of him – alive and well again – was Jesus.

'Peace be with you,' said Jesus. 'See my hands and my side, Thomas. Now stop doubting and believe!'

Thomas fell to his knees and said: 'My Lord and my God!'

Jesus said to him, 'Do you believe because you have seen me? Happy are those who believe but have not seen me!'

Round-up

'Happy are those who believe but have not seen me,' said Jesus. People who are Christians have never seen Jesus with their eyes and yet they believe in him. Most of the time they are happy because they believe Jesus has conquered death – they believe Jesus is their Saviour and friend, so they needn't be afraid.

Prayer

Lord, this Easter time help us to remember what Easter is really all about. You loved us so much that you went through all that for us.
Amen.

Learning

from mistakes

 **Aim**   We all make mistakes. Some people learn from them and move on as better people, but others do not learn from them and seem to make the same mistake over and over again.

Song   One or two words (*Come On, Let's Celebrate*)

 Puppet sketch

John	Hey, Micky, I met Charlie a couple of days ago? (*To the audience*) Charlie is Micky's toddler brother. What a cutie!
Micky	What a cutie? He's being a right Charlie! That's how he is!
John	How do you mean?
Micky	You should see him eating his food. He has far too much on his spoon! It goes everywhere – all over his face and all over his bib. He gets in a right state!
John	Ha, I know someone else who used to be like that.
Micky	Really? The other day, I was doing my homework. I got up and left it for a second, but guess what happened next?
John	It was Charlied!
Micky	Exactly, he scribbled and dribbled all over it!
John	Oh dear. But I know someone else who used to do that sort of thing.
Micky	Ha, no one else could possibly be that bad! I had some friends come round yesterday and we played Jenga.
John	When you have to build a tower as tall as you can without it falling down?
Micky	(*Excitedly*) That's the game! It was really high but then Charlie walked in and guess what?
John	It was Charlied.
Micky	Yeah! He knocked it over!
John	I know someone else who used to do that sort of thing!
Micky	No one could be that bad. Anyway, I'd had enough. I grabbed my bag and put Charlie in it and shouted: 'Mum, I'm just going down to the pet shop to sell Charlie – I won't be long.' But guess what? Mum came rushing in and told me off!
John	Ah, so that's why your mum was so upset when I saw her.

Micky	Was she?
John	Guess what, Micky? You used to make a terrible mess with your food too.
Micky	Me? Never!
John	It's true. And you used to scribble and dribble over things!
Micky	Me? Never!
John	It's true! And you used to love knocking things down just like Charlie! But now you're older you've learnt not to do those sort of things. You've learnt from experience.
Micky	What a clever chap I am!
John	But you're still very good at putting your foot in it.
Micky	What do you mean?
John	Charlie has been keeping your mum awake at night so your mum is tired and needs your support and help with Charlie.
Micky	But instead I just moan about Charlie and even wanted to sell him. No wonder Mum was so upset. I was only joking. I love Charlie really – he's great fun.
John	Great! Tell your mum that. Learn from your mistake and help and support your mum and be careful what you say!

Bible story

Genesis 37-47: Joseph

Have you ever been tempted to sell your brother or sister like Micky was?

There were some brothers in the Bible who did precisely that! They were so fed up with their brother, who obviously thought that he was much better than they were!

One day their brother even said that he'd had a dream about his brothers' sheaves of corn bowing down to his! What a cheek! Did that mean that they were meant to bow down to him and treat him like a king. Huh! No way – dream on!

Their father had given Joseph, that was the boy's name, a really posh and colourful coat that he loved to show off. The brothers hated him so much that when an opportunity came to sell him as a slave they took it! Imagine that – selling your own brother as a slave.

So this boy who had been spoilt all his life suddenly found himself having to work for others, and he was also thrown into prison. He wasn't proud any more. He stopped showing off and stopped expecting people to treat him like a king – he had learnt from his mistakes.

But although everything had gone wrong for Joseph it was all part of God's plan. God was looking after him and one day the king himself sent for Joseph! The king had a dream and he wanted Joseph to tell him what his dream meant.

God told Joseph what the dream was and what it meant, and suddenly Joseph became the hero because he warned the king that there was going to be a famine that would last for seven years so they stored up plenty of food. Joseph saved the day and he became a very powerful man!

One day a group of men all came and bowed at his feet. They had travelled many miles and were begging to buy some food to take back to their family. Yep, you guessed it! It was Joseph's brothers – those same brothers who had sold him into slavery.

Joseph could have put them to death for doing such a wicked thing to him but instead he forgave them. He had realised it was all part of God's plan to save his people. Joseph had learnt from his mistakes and so had his brothers, who were so sorry for what they had done to him.

Round-up

Some people never learn from their mistakes and they make the same mistakes – time after time, after time! We all make mistakes! We need to realise and accept that we've made mistakes and learn from them, making us better people.

Prayer

Father God, thank you for this wonderful story about Joseph. Thank you that he was able to forgive his brothers and learn from his mistakes. Please help us to do the same.
Amen.

Messed up big time

 **Aim**

To show how God made this wonderful planet and made humans in his image. But we messed up and sin came into the world – and we've been messed up ever since and missed out.

Song

Image of God (*Come On, Let's Celebrate*)

 Puppet sketch

John	Micky, how did your circus skills workshop go last night? (*To audience*) Micky has joined this special club which teaches him to juggle, spin plates and other exciting things.
Micky	Not too bad.
John	I heard . . .
Micky	(*Interrupting*) What have you heard?
John	What? Oh, I heard that you were trying to learn the unicycle.
Micky	I don't want to talk about it.
John	Oh dear. Something happened, didn't it? Come on, you can tell me.
Micky	Nice weather!
John	Oh, dear! Now I know something has happened!
Micky	How?
John	Because you're trying to change the subject. Come on, how did you get on?
Micky	Carefully!
John	Look, you know what I mean. Something happened, didn't it?
Micky	Sort of. I managed to do ever so well on the unicycle. The clown teacher was most impressed. He said that I had a good sense of balance!
John	So what went wrong?
Micky	The clown teacher said we had to leave the equipment for a short while because he was going to the kitchen to make us all a cup of orange. Everybody did as he said apart from me. I thought I had mastered the unicycle and so I had another go. I was doing fine when suddenly I lost control. Just then, guess who walked through the door balancing a tray of cups on his head!
John	Oh, no!

Micky	Yes, you've guessed it. I went straight into him, knocking the clown teacher and cups flying! So we had one very wet and sticky clown. He was not a happy chappy! But it all happened so fast that he hadn't seen who had done it.
John	You did own up, didn't you?
Micky	He shouted: 'Who did that?' I was scared! So I thought it was safer to keep quiet.
John	Micky!
Micky	I tried to blame someone else at first, but I did own up eventually!
John	What happened?
Micky	He's banned me. For two whole weeks I'm not allowed to go! I'm missing out because I disobeyed him. He told me how dangerous the equipment was and he wasn't sure he could trust me any more.
John	He's right! You'll have to prove to him that he can trust you again! Then maybe you won't miss out any more!
Micky	You're right! I'll never do anything wrong again, because you miss out when you do! Bye!

Bible story

Genesis 3 – Adam and Eve

Wow! Can you image what it must have been like to be the first man God ever created! The whole world all to yourself! Just you and all the animals – and they were all friendly in those days!

God made a special garden that he called the Garden of Eden! Wow! It was a brilliant place, full of beautiful trees with amazing leaves and fruit, a stream to relax by, birds singing their songs and all the animals!

The man was put in charge of them all! God gave the first man the name Adam and it says that God actually used to walk in the garden with Adam. I wonder what sort of things they used to chat about?

Then God created a woman called Eve. At first it was wonderful – they all walked together in the garden. But I forgot to mention one of the trees. Adam and Eve had thousands of wonderful fruit trees to enjoy but God said there was just one tree he didn't want them to eat from – it was called 'the tree of the Knowledge of Good and Evil'.

But guess what? One day they had another visitor – a snake. The snake said to Eve: 'Why don't you try the fruit of that tree – it looks really yummy!' 'Oh no' said Eve, 'That's the tree of the Knowledge of Good and Evil and if we eat that then we will die!' 'Die?' said the snake. 'You won't die. God doesn't want you to eat it because he knows if you do then you will be as clever as him. Go on – have a bite!'

Fancy listening to a snake rather than obeying God, but that's what she did – she took a bite of the fruit and then passed it on to Adam and they ate together.

God came for a walk in the garden with Adam and Eve but they were hiding.

'Where are you?' said God. 'We're hiding,' they said. They had never had to hide before so they weren't very good at it.

'Why are you hiding?' said God.

'Well, because we're naked!' they said.

'Naked? Who told you that you were naked? Have you eaten from the tree that I commanded you not to eat from?' God asked.

'Er, yes,' said Adam. 'It was Eve's fault. She persuaded me!'

See, straight away they started to blame each other. God had set them one little test to see if humans would obey and love him and whether he could trust them or not. Out of all the thousands of beautiful fruit trees, they ate from the one they weren't allowed to eat from and messed up.

From then on they never walked with God in the garden any more. In fact, they didn't live in the garden any more, because God didn't trust them. They had messed up big time!

Round-up

Humans have messed things up ever since. We've messed up big time and then often blame others for our mistakes. We often make the wrong choices but God does forgive us and will help us not to make those mistakes again if we ask him to.

Prayer

Dear Father God, sorry for all the times we mess things up. Please forgive us and help us to do what is right.
Amen.

Missed out!

 **Aim**

Often we miss out on things because we may be nervous or because we are lazy!

Song

Nobody's a nobody (*Come On, Let's Celebrate*)

 Puppet sketch

John	Hey Micky, how did you get on in McDonald's?
Micky	How did you know about McDonald's?
John	We set up the date for you! (*To audience*) There's this girl that Micky really likes called . . .
Micky	(*Interrupting*) Lovely Liz with the lovely lips!
John	And for some reason, she likes him too! So Micky's mates and Lizzy's mates set up a surprise meeting in McDonald's!
Micky	Wow! I couldn't believe my eyes! I walked into McDonald's and there she was, sitting at a table on her own! I went across and asked if I could join her!
John	That was very polite! How did you get on?
Micky	I saw her beautiful golden hair and I was going to say: 'I love your golden hair,' but I was nervous and it came out as 'I love your plastic chair!' She looked at me strange-like!
John	I'm not surprised!
Micky	I saw her lovely lips and I decided I was going to be brave and ask her for a kiss but it came out all wrong! I said: 'I'd love to nick your chips!'
John	Oh dear!
Micky	I thought I'd try one more time and ask her for a date! But it came out all wrong again! I said: 'Will you go out with my mate!' She ran off! I suppose she went to find my mate to ask him out!
John	Oh dear, I'm sorry to hear about that. But Micky, where were you in the afternoon. You said: 'I'll meet you at four in the pool!' I was looking forward to having a swim but you never turned up!
Micky	Oh, I couldn't be bothered. I was too upset!
John	Well thanks a lot! You let me down! You could have phoned! I was there on my own! Actually, I wasn't because guess who turned up?

Micky	No idea and I don't really care!
John	I think you do! It was lovely Liz with the lovely lips!
Micky	What?!? I bet she was with my mate!
John	No, she was on her own. We got chatting and she told me that she really likes you and was so pleased to see you in McDonald's but you were just being daft, saying lots of silly things that didn't make sense!
Micky	She really likes me?
John	Yes! You missed out on seeing her all because you were lazy and selfish.
Micky	(*Looking really down!*) Don't rub it in!
John	But I'm sure it's not too late! She's waiting for you in McDonald's. (*Or in place relevant to your location*)
Micky	Excellent! (*He disappears*)
John	Cor! He is keen!

Bible story	Luke 19:11-26 – The gold coins!

Jesus told this story. There was a very rich and important man. He was going away to a distant country so he called in his servants.

'Servants! Come here! I'm going away to a distant country!'

'Oh, that's nice – a holiday is it?' one of the servants may have said.

'No, no, no! I'm going to be made a king! But before I go I want to give each of you servants a gold coin!' the boss replied. And he gave each of them a gold coin. 'See what you can earn with this!' he said. And off he went on his journey.

You can just imagine the servants chatting, can't you. 'What are you going to do, then?'

'Don't know, it sounds too much like hard work to me!' said one. 'Sounds like a challenge to me!' said another! And off they went their separate ways to see what they could earn . . . or did they?

After some time the rich man returned. He was now a proud and powerful king!

'Now where are those servants of mine?' he thought and he sent for the first servant. 'I gave you a gold coin. What have you done with it?'

The first servant was very nervous as he approached his new king. 'Well your Majesty, here's your gold coin. I worked really hard from morning to night and here's ten more gold coins!' he said. 'Well done, my good and faithful servant! Because you have proved what a hard worker and reliable person you are I'm going to put you in charge of ten cities!' said the king. 'What? Me! Wow! Excellent! I'm an important man!' the first servant said with delight.

The second servant came in, looking worried. 'Well, I gave you a gold coin. What did you do with that coin?' said the king. 'Here is your coin,' said the second servant. 'I worked really hard – honest – and here's five more gold coins!' he said.

'Well done, my good and faithful servant,' said the king. 'I will put you in charge of five cities!'

He sent for the third servant and in he strolled! 'Here's your gold coin,' he said. 'I'll be off, then.'

'What's this?' said the king.

'It's a gold coin!' said the servant. 'You should know – you gave it to me. Perhaps a little more grubby, because I buried it, you see, but at least it's back safe and sound!'

The king was angry and said: 'Why didn't you put it in the bank? I could have at least collected the interest. You lazy servant!' And, turning to his attendants, he said: 'Take it away from him and give it to the one who has ten. Take him away – I don't want that lazy servant in my kingdom!'

Round-up

Some people show great promise at something. They could be good at a particular sport or something else, but they never get anywhere with it, sometimes because they lack self-confidence or sometimes because they are simply lazy and can't be bothered!

Prayer

Dear Lord, help us to realise that we are all special and can all do different things! Help us not to be lazy and to do our best in all that we do.
Amen.

Never give up!

 Aim

To show how Jesus had a task to do. It was a difficult task and he could have given up or even cheated but he didn't.

Songs

For God so loved the world (*Come On, Let's Celebrate*)
Come on, let's celebrate (*Come On, Let's Celebrate*)
At the name of Jesus (*Bible Explosion*)

 Puppet sketch

John	Well done, Micky! (*To audience*) He has just completed a seven-mile fun run!
Micky	I'm totally worn out, but it was worth it in the end! I raised lots of money for charity.
John	Was it hard?
Micky	Of course! But (*name of mate*) made it even harder!
John	Why?
Micky	When I told him I was going to run seven miles he laughed at me and bet me 10 quid I couldn't do it.
John	Gosh!
Micky	I said why don't you give me the £10 for the charity if I make it!
John	That's a lot of money!
Micky	I know! I was only joking! He just laughed and said 'OK!' He didn't think I had a chance so he wasn't worried about paying up.
John	What happened?
Micky	The race started, I paced myself well. But it was a hot day and he didn't think I would last! But when I came down to the last mile he started to look very worried! I was really shattered but I wasn't going to give up. He tried to distract me!
John	What! How?
Micky	He ran alongside me and asked me if I wanted to get a cool ice cream at his house! Cor, I was tempted.
John	Oh no – you didn't, did you?
Micky	No, I realised just in time that he was trying to tempt me so he wouldn't have to pay me the £10.

John	That was a close one!
Micky	Then he ran alongside me again and told me that Delicious Debbie, the babe from year six, wanted to go out with me and wanted to see me now! My heart started pounding even more! Could it be true? Then I realised! He was trying to trick me. She doesn't even know my name!
John	That was mean!
Micky	Yep! Then he told me that running was for wimps and wasn't cool, and that I looked like a fool! That hurt! But I wasn't giving up!
John	Anyway, that's not true!
Micky	Exactly! He tried one or two other things like: 'There's a bus coming! Jump on it, you'll finish quicker then.' But I told him I'm not a cheat! He asked me if I wanted to have a go on his Gameboy? 'No!' I said, really firmly. Finally, he gave up!
John	What? He knew he couldn't persuade you?
Micky	No, he couldn't keep up! He was too shattered! But I made it! I didn't cheat, and I wasn't tempted off course!
John	A champion! Well done! Did he pay up?
Micky	No, I haven't seen him since, but it doesn't matter because I still made some money for charity – but the main thing was I made it! I ran seven miles! Amazing, or what!
John	Yes, excellent!

Bible story Luke 24:50 and Acts 1:1-12 – The Ascension of Jesus

A champion climbs the podium for all to see and receives the medal for finishing the race.

Did you know that when the leading runner in a marathon enters the stadium all the other events stop and everyone in the stadium cheers as the champion completes the last lap? What an atmosphere!

Then finally the champion climbs the podium to receive their medal. They have done it! Everyone honours them for their fantastic achievement!

It was like this with Jesus. He had finished the race, and done what God had asked him to do. He had come in order to tell everyone – whether, rich or poor, black or white, young or old – that God loves them and sees them as his children and wants them to put their trust in him.

But not everyone liked this message! They thought they were more important than other people and that they were God's children! And anyway, how dare Jesus talk like this, he makes it sound like he knows God better than anyone else!

So they had Jesus arrested. Jesus was powerful – he had shown by all the wonderful miracles he performed that he could have called down the angels from heaven who would rescue him and show that he really was the Son of God. But that wasn't God's plan, so Jesus was taken and put to death on the cross. When he died on the cross he took the blame for all the wrong things we say and do. But that's not the end of the story – oh no – in one sense it's just the beginning. You see, he came back to life again! What a champion!

About 40 days after Jesus had risen from the dead Jesus and his friends went to the hill called the Mount of Olives. As he was talking to the disciples he seemed to be getting taller! Jesus' feet had actually left the ground and he was rising into the air!

His friends watched open-mouthed as Jesus gradually went higher and higher, until finally he disappeared into the clouds! Suddenly, two men dressed in white appeared from nowhere and said: 'Men of Galilee, why are you looking up into the sky?'

'Jesus has gone back to heaven, but don't be sad, because one day he'll come back again.'

Round-up

The end of the race. Jesus had run the race and stayed on the right track. He had never given up. He had succeeded and, like a champion athlete climbing the podium to receive his prize, Jesus was lifted up to heaven to take up his prize as the ultimate champion.

Even though it was tough, Jesus never gave up and we should never give up doing what is right – even though sometimes it may seem easier to cheat and do what is wrong.

Prayer

Father God, thank you that Jesus never gave up, and that he became a champion. Help us to never give up doing what we know is right.
Amen.

No short cuts

Aim To show that there are no short cuts! If you want to do well at something and succeed you have to work at it and try hard. But it's worth it in the end!

Song Keep yourself in training (*Come On, Let's Celebrate*)

Puppet sketch

John	Hey Micky! I saw your mate Tango the other day and he said you were going to run in the 100 metres race. Did you?
Micky	Yes, I did!
John	He said you were very confident. In fact you said that you were bound to win! Why were you so confident? Do you do any running?
Micky	Yes, every day! I run for the bus!
John	Is that it?
Micky	Of course not! I've got a secret weapon!
John	Secret weapon? I don't like the sound of that! You didn't cheat, did you?
Micky	Of course not! I have -------- trainers! (*Name of a top make of trainers*)
John	What on earth are they?
Micky	What? You've never heard of them? They are only the best trainers you can buy! They cost a fortune! All the top athletes have them and win!
John	Well, how did you get on?
Micky	What do you mean?
John	In the race. Did you win?
Micky	Not quite.
John	Second?
Micky	Not exactly.
John	Third?
Micky	Nice weather for this time of year!
John	Last?
Micky	Yes! I don't understand. All the top athletes have them and win! But I came last!
John	Those top athletes are top athletes because of all the training and hard work they put in, not because they wear top gear!

Micky	What? Why didn't anyone tell me that before! I'd better go and start training for next year!

Bible story

1 Corinthians 9:25 and Hebrews 12:1

You could dress up in wellington boots and overcoat. Ask the question, 'What do you think I'm getting ready for?'

Wait for a response. The answer: A race! Would I win?

An athlete wouldn't dress up in wellington boots and an overcoat for a race. They have to be prepared to give up certain things like certain types of food. They have to be committed, giving up time to practise in all kinds of weather.

2 Timothy 4:6-8

Living a Christian life and a good life is like running in a race. Certain things are bad for you – things like selfishness, being greedy and pride. We need to put others first.

Round-up

It's not the winning that counts, it's the taking part and the finishing. To be able to say 'I made it!' and to receive a reward.

Prayer

Lord, help us as we live our lives to be fair and to train and work hard. *Amen.*

One or two words

Ideal date	Around Bonfire Night.
Aim	Fire can scar for life. So can the tongue. The aim is to help children see the importance in being careful in what they say.
Song	One or two words (*Come On, Let's Celebrate*)
Puppet sketch	
Micky	Hey, John! Do you want to play a game?
John	What sort of game?
Micky	A guessing game. Guess the object. I'll give you some clues and you have to see if you can guess what the object is. If you can't guess then I'll see if this lot can guess! (*Indicating the audience*)
John	OK, go for it.
Micky	Here goes. Clue number one . . . it's anything from five to ten centimetres long.
John	No idea.
Micky	Second clue . . . it's slimy or wet.
John	A worm!
Micky	No. Third clue . . . it lives in a sort of cave with an entrance that opens and closes at one end and a tunnel at the other end.
John	A bear!
Micky	I think bears are bigger than that! Fourth clue . . . it can be used as a nasty weapon!
John	This is getting harder!
Micky	Fifth clue . . . everyone has one!
John	I haven't got a clue!
Micky	It's pink!
John	A pink weapon that lives in a sort of cave, is slimy, is five to ten centimetres long and everyone has one.
Micky	Do you give up?
John	Yes, unless they can guess! (*Looking at audience*)

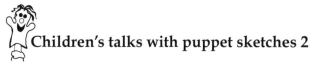

Micky	I'll show you mine! (*Sticks out his tongue*) A tongue! I beat you!
John	That's not fair! How can you say a tongue is a nasty weapon? You can't hit me with it!
Micky	I've never told you this before, but you are a real idiot. Fancy not knowing the answer. Plus you need your hair cut, you're a real scruff and you smell.
John	Micky! That's not a very nice thing to say. I thought we were meant to be friends. You're normally such a nice chap! (*Pause*) Oh, I get it! The tongue can be a nasty weapon if you say horrible things that can hurt.
Micky	Yes, you can use your tongue to praise people and say encouraging, pleasant things, or you can use it in a bad way. I need to go now, but remember – use the tongue to say good things and not bad.

Illustration

(*Show a match and a tongue*)

What do they have in common?

1) One little spark can burn down a whole forest.
2) One little tongue can do a lot of damage like spreading rumours, nasty remarks, exciting a crowd (We are the greatest! You're a load of rubbish!)

You may have heard the saying 'Sticks and stones may break my bones, but names will never hurt me!'

Bible story

James 3:5, 6

Words can hurt, upset, lead to anger and sometimes do permanent damage, just like a fire can burn and scar for life.

James, a man in the Bible, said: 'You can use the tongue for good, to praise God, or you can use the tongue for bad, to destroy.' He also said: 'People have learnt to tame all kinds of animals, but they can't control their tongue.'

Round-up

It's coming up to Bonfire Night, a time when many of us will have fireworks. Let's be very, very careful because although fireworks are beautiful they are also dangerous and can scar for life. So follow the Firework Code and stand well back, and let a responsible adult light the fireworks.

But what we say to people can also scar for life. So don't be mean and horrible, but be kind and encourage one another.

Remember this – '*Zip up your mouth if you're going to put someone down but unzip it if you're going to build them up.*'

Prayer

Lord, we know that we need to be careful of fire. Help us to remember to be careful in what we say to people.

Amen.

Overlooked

 Aim   To show how important it is to include everyone. It's important to look out for those who may be overlooked, for whatever reason.

Song   V.I.P. (*Come On, Let's Celebrate*)

 Puppet sketch

John	Hey, Micky, I heard a story about you that I find hard to believe.
Micky	What's that then?
John	That you, you of all people, went on a sponsored silence!
Micky	Yes, that's true. What's so amazing about that?
John	How long did you last? Thirty seconds?
Micky	Cheek! A lot longer than that!
John	What, five minutes?
Micky	No, longer.
John	Thirty minutes? One hour? What – even longer?
Micky	Yes! I lasted two whole school days!
John	Wow! I'm impressed and amazed! If I give you some money now, will you do it again. It would be nice to have a bit of peace and quiet!
Micky	Cheek! I'll never ever do it again!
John	Why?
Micky	Well, at first everyone chatted to me, trying to make me talk, but when they found out I was so determined to keep quiet they gave up.
John	Good. That was a bit mean of them.
Micky	They stopped talking to me completely because I didn't talk back, and then they started to leave me out of things like games and saving me a place at dinner time. It was horrible being ignored and overlooked.
John	I bet you made up for it when you were allowed to talk again!
Micky	I sure did!
John	You know, Micky, there are a lot of people who are left out of things and ignored, or overlooked all the time. Maybe it's because they are quiet, or different in some way. So everyone ignores them and leaves them out day after day.
Micky	That must be really terrible.

Children's talks with puppet sketches 2

John	Yes, so if you can think of anyone like that then try and include them in things and talk to them, however hard it may be.
Micky	Good idea! I can think of someone like that now. I'm going to go and invite them round. Bye!

Bible story

Mark 10:46-52 – Blind Bartimaeus

What am I doing? (*Mime begging*) There were a lot of beggars in Jesus' time.

Bartimaeus was blind. In those days this meant that no-one would give him a job, so he would have to sit on the side of the road and beg for money. People would try to ignore beggars. They were a nuisance and so they were overlooked and ignored.

People who are blind use their other senses far more. The senses of smell and hearing. Bartimaeus had heard about a man named Jesus, who had made blind people see.

'I wish I could see him,' Bartimaeus thought to himself, 'but I can't because I'm blind.'

One day he heard the noise of a large crowd of people coming along the street. He sensed the excitement. Someone special was coming his way. He heard them call out to Jesus. Could it be the same Jesus who could make blind people see?

When the crowd got closer Bartimaeus couldn't contain his excitement. He started to shout: 'Jesus! Jesus, Son of David, take pity on me!'

The crowd told him to be quiet, but he wouldn't. He shouted again, even louder this time.

'Jesus, Son of David, take pity on me!'

Jesus stopped and said: 'Call him.'

Bartimaeus threw off his cloak, jumped up and came to Jesus.

'What do you want me to do for you?' Jesus asked him.

'Teacher,' Bartimaeus answered, 'I want to see again.'

'Go,' said Jesus. 'Your faith has made you well.'

At once Bartimaeus was able to see and he followed Jesus on the road.

Round-up

The crowd told the beggar to be quiet, but Jesus didn't. He had time for him. We need to make time for people. Don't ignore or overlook people.

Prayer

Lord, help us to notice people who may be overlooked so that we can invite them to join in whatever is going on.
Amen.

Sheep don't
follow strangers

Aim To show that we have to be careful who we trust and that we should never go with strangers.

Song Image of God (*Come On, Let's Celebrate*)

Puppet sketch

Micky	I can't wait until this evening!
John	Why? What are you doing?
Micky	I'm going out!
John	Where?
Micky	Out to the fair! I like the roller-coaster best – up and down, round and round. (*Move puppet to the action*)
John	Where is the fair? I didn't know there was a fair locally.
Micky	Nor did I!
John	Who are you going with?
Micky	This very kind man.
John	Who?
Micky	He's got a nice smile.
John	Who?
Micky	He's very generous. He gave me sweets!
John	What's his name?
Micky	Mr Niceguy!
John	That's a strange name! How long have you known him?
Micky	Ages!
John	How long is ages?
Micky	He walked with me on the way to school and he said he had chosen me to be his special friend, then he gave me an invitation to go to the fair with him.
John	So, Micky, you don't really know him, do you?
Micky	No, not really. But he seems very nice.
John	Yes, but he might not be! I'm pleased you told me about him. I think I ought to meet him, too!
Micky	Good idea!

John	You know, you should never go off with strangers, however nice they may seem!
Micky	Can I go to the fair with you instead then?
John	Definitely! If there is a local fair.
Micky	I'll go and get ready!

Bible story

John 10:1-18

Have you ever seen sheep eating grass in a field? Have you ever tried to walk up to one of those sheep? If so then they probably ran away! But if the shepherd walked into the field they wouldn't run away. In fact they would run to him.

Just imagine being a little sheep. You love your shepherd very much because he has always looked after you. He's taken you to green pastures and still waters so you can drink from the stream. But today he starts to lead you along a new path. It's scary, full of strange noises and cold shadows. What do you do? Do you think to yourself: 'The shepherd has taken the wrong path,' and choose to run away, or do you choose to get as close to the shepherd as possible and trust him to lead you through to green pastures! You see, there was a reason for him leading you along that path. It was to find fresh, green grass. It's a good job the sheep trust and love the shepherd so much.

Round-up

The sheep know the shepherd – that's why they trust him even when the path gets rough. In the same way God wants us to trust him and allow him to lead us, even though sometimes the path seems rough. We can trust God because he is like a shepherd to us, but unfortunately we can't trust everyone – so don't follow strangers.

Prayer

Lord, thank you for people who love us and care for us. Thank you that you are like a good shepherd, and please help us to trust you. Lord, I pray that we will be careful not to follow strangers.
Amen.

Use your brains!

 Aim

Apparently humans have big brains, but if that's the case then we often don't use them. The aim is to get people to think for themselves and use their brains, not just follow the crowd!

Song

Image of God (*Come On, Let's Celebrate*)

Puppet sketch

Micky	Today's theme is 'Use your brains' but I don't think I can talk about that!
John	Why?
Micky	'Cause I haven't got any!
John	What?
Micky	Brains!
John	Of course you have!
Micky	Well, my dad once said that if I had any brains then I'd be dangerous!
John	Oh, that's just your dad trying to be funny! Of course you've got brains!
Micky	I wish I could be like my little sister – she's got brains coming out of her ears! She is so brainy! The other day I was struggling with my homework and my little sister said: 'Let's have a look,' and then said: 'Easy-peazy lemon squeezy!' and did my homework just like that!
John	Yeah, she is a clever little girl, but I heard that you used your brains the other day! You're the hero, that's what I heard!
Micky	(*Looking confused*) I am?
John	Yeah! Tango said that you scared off three or four bullies the other day!
Micky	(*Still confused*) I did?
John	Yes! They were picking on Tango but when you came round the corner they all ran off!
Micky	Oh that! It wasn't anything brave. I walked round the corner and saw them picking on Tango. I thought if I tried to help I'd get hurt too. So I walked off!
John	(*Looking confused*) You did?
Micky	I went back round the corner, then in a big, loud voice I said: 'Oh, hello, Mr Jones.' He's the headteacher! As soon as the bullies heard that they ran off!

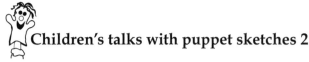
John	Wow, good thinking! So you pretended Mr Jones was there.
Micky	Well he was, sort of. Actually he was on the other side of the playground, but they didn't know that. Good job they can't see round corners!
John	Excellent! You used your brains and saved the day!
Micky	Oh wow! I did, didn't I! I've got to go and tell my dad I've got a brain after all! Bye!

Bible story

John 8:1-11 – The woman who was unfaithful

This is a story about how Jesus' wisdom and compassion saved a woman's life.

Jesus was a very popular teacher. Whenever he spoke, the crowds flocked to hear him. But not everyone liked Jesus! For example, the teachers of the law and the Pharisees didn't like Jesus at all! They didn't believe that he was the Son of God and they didn't like his stories.

But worst of all they were jealous that crowds of people flocked to hear him and not them any more. So they plotted to get rid of Jesus! They wanted to trap Jesus and catch him out and make him look a fool.

You can just imagine them coming up with their plan! 'Excellent idea! There's no way out of that one. It's a perfect trap.' They said to each other: 'We'll make Jesus look like a fool!'

They were going to find a woman. A woman who had been caught being unfaithful to her husband!

Back in their time and culture this was considered to be a terrible sin – a very bad thing indeed – and their law said she must be stoned to death!

Not very nice, I agree, but that was their law!

And that's exactly what these bad guys did – they found a woman who had been unfaithful to her husband and dragged her in front of Jesus and said: 'Teacher, this woman was caught being unfaithful to her husband. And that's bad! (*Thumbs down*)

(*To audience*) What is it? Bad (*Get the audience to turn their thumbs down with you*) In fact, it's very bad! (*Turn down thumbs together again*) Now according to the Law of Moses she should be put to death! What do you say we should do, Jesus?'

Now Jesus knew it was a trap and that they were trying to catch him out! He knew that if he said: 'Let her go!' the people would say that Jesus was encouraging them to break the law! But if he said: 'Stone her,' how could he say such a thing, and allow them to kill her like this? It was a good trap! There was no way out for Jesus – or so they thought.

But Jesus bent over and wrote on the ground with his finger! 'What's he doing?' the crowd must have thought.

Then he looked up at the Pharisees, the teachers of the law and the crowd and said: 'Let him who has committed no sin throw the first stone.' Oh, wow!

What a clever answer. You see, it says in the Bible that we've all sinned, done things wrong, and everyone knew that and nobody was going to argue.

One by one all those who had stones in their hands dropped them and quietly left. Then Jesus said to the woman. 'Where are they? Is there anyone left to condemn you?'

'They've all gone!' she said.

Then Jesus said: 'I don't condemn you, either. Go and do not sin again!'

What a brilliant story, because Jesus didn't just follow the crowd. He stopped to think, he used his brain and came up with an amazing answer and saved the lady's life!

Round-up   Humans have huge brains, so let's learn to stop and think, to use our brains and not just follow the crowd, especially when the crowd is wrong. We also need to help others and show compassion just like Jesus did!

Prayer   Thank you, Lord, that you've given us all brains to think with. Help us to use them and choose to do what is right.
Amen.

What a party!

 Aim

To show how Jesus is missed out of the Christmas celebration and is not invited to his own birthday party.

Songs

Band of angels (*Come On, Let's Celebrate*)
Celebration, celebration (*Bible Explosion*)

 Puppet sketch

Micky	Hey, John! Did you enjoy the party?
John	What party?
Micky	Yes! What a party!
John	Micky! What party?
Micky	Wasn't the clown funny!
John	There was a clown?
Micky	And there were great games!
John	Oh what!
Micky	The disco was a laugh, watching Andy dance! (*Wobble puppet as though dancing!*)
John	Sounds like you had a great time!
Micky	Of course! But the food was the best. All that chocolate cake!
John	Who was there?
Micky	What do you mean who was there? You know who was there! Andy, Steve, Paul, Rachel, all your best mates and your mum and dad and family!
John	What?
Micky	So, John! Did you enjoy your surprise birthday party!
John	A surprise birthday party? I didn't have a party!
Micky	Yes you did!
John	Well, no one invited me!
Micky	Oops! I knew I forgot to invite somebody!
John	Micky! Hang on. Let me get this straight. You organised a surprise party for me. You had a funny clown, a disco, games, wonderful food – you invited all my best mates and family!
Micky	Yep!

John	But you forgot to invite me!
Micky	Er, yes! Sorry!
John	Thanks a lot. I missed out because you forgot to invite me to my own birthday party!
Micky	I've just had a brilliant idea! I'm going to organise a wonderful party and you will be the first one I'll invite! I'd better go! I've got a party to organise! Bye!
John	(*To audience*) Fancy having a birthday party and forgetting to invite the one whose birthday it is! Whose birthday do we celebrate at Christmas? (*Jesus'!*) But so many people forget all about him and completely miss him out of the Christmas celebration!

Bible story

Luke 2:18-20

When you were a newborn baby I bet your dad was on the phone within seconds, telling people the good news. I bet he told your grandma and grandad, brothers and sisters, friends and neighbours.

But I bet he didn't go down to the local building site and invite all the builders to come and see you – they would have been gobsmacked if he had!

But that's exactly what God did when Jesus was born. He sent his angel to invite – not friends and family – a bunch of tough-guy shepherds.

Do you think they were interested in knowing that a baby was born? They sure were! They would have been amazed that God had invited them, because most people in those days didn't think shepherds were very important. But God did, and he invited them to see the most amazing and important baby ever born – God's only Son!

Wow! They didn't hesitate at all, even though they were busy looking after their sheep. Maybe the angels looked after the sheep while they were gone – they would have had no trouble from wild animals. Immediately, the shepherds went to celebrate the birth of this wonderful baby boy.

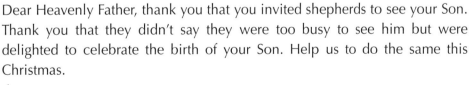

Round-up

People are often so busy getting ready for Christmas they forget all about Jesus! They miss out on what Christmas is really all about!

Prayer

Dear Heavenly Father, thank you that you invited shepherds to see your Son. Thank you that they didn't say they were too busy to see him but were delighted to celebrate the birth of your Son. Help us to do the same this Christmas.
Amen.

Which way?

 **Aim** Sometimes we need guidance to know what is right, or to know which way to go. Christians believe that God will guide us in our lives and that the Bible is a bit like a map, showing us the right way to go.

Songs Image of God (*Come On, Let's Celebrate*)
Trust in the Lord (*Come On, Let's Celebrate*)

 **Puppet sketch**

Micky	John, I need some guidance. I don't know what to do.
John	In what sense?
Micky	Homework.
John	I won't guide you to the right answers, if that's what you were hoping!
Micky	No, I've got to write about what I want to be when I grow up.
John	What ideas have you had?
Micky	A brain surgeon! I think I would be good at that!
John	A brain surgeon? Micky, you need a brain for that!
Micky	Oi!
John	Only joking! But I do have doubts about that idea. Any other ideas?
Micky	A male model!
John	But you have to be good looking for that!
Micky	Exactly! Or maybe I could be a pop star!
John	You need to be able to sing for that!
Micky	Watch it!
John	What do you like doing the best?
Micky	Climbing trees!
John	Yes! Where do you like going best? The city, or the countryside?
Micky	The countryside!
John	Do you like being indoors or outdoors?
Micky	Both, but my favourite place is outside!
John	Maybe you could be a farmer, or maybe a forest ranger! You love nature, you love the outdoors, animals and trees!
Micky	Excellent idea. Thanks for your guidance! Bye!

Illustration

Draw out some road signs from the Highway Code.

All of these signs are there to guide us when we are on the road. They warn us of danger, tell us which way to go and how fast to travel.

The Bible is like God's guidebook. It tells us the right road to take, warns us of danger and tells us how to live our lives.

Bible story

Luke 6:12-13

The other way God guides us is when we ask him to, through prayer. Even Jesus, God's own Son, knew how important it was to ask God for guidance. One day he had a very important choice to make. He wanted to know who to choose to be his disciples, people who would help in the work God wanted him to do.

So he didn't ask his friends or a Sunday school teacher, or even the minister – he asked God! He went up a mountain and prayed and then the next morning he chose his disciples!

Round-up

Right through our lives we have to make important choices, such as what job we will do, where we will live and who we might marry. Sometimes it's good to ask people what they think we should do, but Christians believe we can and should always ask God to guide us!

Prayer

Lord, thank you for those who guide us. Help us to realise we can ask you for guidance. Please guide us in the right path to choose.
Amen.

Wow! What a great place!

Aim

To show how wonderful our planet is and how God made humans the caretakers – which means we need to look after it and make sure we share the produce we get from it. Are we 'caretakers', or just 'takers'?

Songs

Variety, variety (*Come On, Let's Celebrate*)
Down in the jungle (*Come On, Let's Celebrate*)

Puppet sketch

(*Everyone calls for Micky, but when he appears he is down in the dumps, looking very sorry for himself*)

John	What's up?
Micky	Nothing much. I'm just a bit sad, that's all.
John	Micky, that's not like you.
Micky	I've just been to the shop and I've got my photos back from my holiday.
John	Oh, dear. Didn't they turn out?
Micky	Yes, they all did.
John	Oh, well, what's up then?
Micky	It reminded me of what happened on holiday. Ralph, Tango and I all made a fantastic, huge sandcastle. (*He looks up to the ceiling to show how big it was*)
John	Cor! That big?
Micky	Yes, we made a big mountain of sand and put a sandcastle on top! (*Micky is gradually getting more excited*) Then we dug a moat round it and filled it with seawater. Then we got a big stone for the drawbridge, then built a wall around our sandcastle!
John	Wow! That sounds fantastic! Have you got a photo of it?
Micky	No! The three of us went to get the camera, but when we returned it had gone!
John	Gone? Gone where? Had the sea come in?
Micky	No.
John	Maybe you were on the wrong part of the beach.
Micky	No. There were four lads having a lot of fun dancing on the beach.
John	Dancing?

Micky	Yes, on top of our sandcastle! Ralph was mad! He chased them. (*He looks down*) All that hard work. We had been working on it all day and we were very pleased with it. But it only took them a few seconds to smash it down. Why did they do it?
John	I don't know. My mum once had wonderful flowers in her garden. She looked after them and they were very beautiful. Then suddenly we saw a dog trampling them all down. They were ruined! She was very upset.
Micky	Why do people ruin things that don't belong to them? Don't they realise it upsets people?
John	I really don't know the answer to that. Let's make sure we never do anything like that and look after things. (*Micky is still down in the dumps, so John turns to the audience*) Let's tell him we reckon he's a real cool dude of a monkey! All together! Micky, you're a real cool dude of a monkey!
Micky	(*Looks up and jigs around*) Thanks! I've got to go and finish looking at my photos! Bye!

Bible story

Matthew 21:33-41 – The vineyard

Jesus told a story in the Bible which is very similar to this.

There was a man who owned some land. He decided he would turn it into a vineyard. This meant lots of hard work! He would have to dig the land and plant the vine. (*Mime digging and planting*)

He lived in a hot country, so it would be very hot work. (*Mime mopping brow*)

Then he probably thought to himself: 'I ought to put a fence round my vineyard, so no one will steal what is mine.'

That would have been a big job. It could have taken days. Then he dug a big hole for a winepress. It was all very hard work! As the vine grew he would have realised that he couldn't see across the top of the vines. So he built a watchtower, once again a very hard and tiring job. At last he had really finished!

He had to go and work away, so he asked some men to look after the vineyard for him, to become caretakers. After a while the landowner must have become quite excited. He would have thought: 'It must be time for harvest!'

So he sent a servant to go and collect his share, but the tenants wouldn't give him anything. They just beat him up and sent him back to the landowner.

'Why did they do such a thing?' asked the landowner. 'I only want my share.'

So he sent another servant. But this time they took him and beat him to death. The message got back to the landowner.

'How dare they treat my servants like this!' said the landowner. 'Have they forgotten who owns the vineyard? What shall I do? I shall send my own, dear son. Surely they will respect him!'

But when the tenants saw him they said to one another: 'This is the owner's son. Let's kill him and his property will be ours!'

And that's what they did.

Then the landowner went with an army and killed them and put others in charge of his vineyard.

Round-up

It says in the Bible that God has put us humans in charge of this wonderful planet, Earth. Let's not be like the tenants in the story, being greedy and selfish. We need to look after it and share it with other people in other countries. We also need to look after the animals. Let's be good caretakers and not just takers. We need to look after this beautiful planet.

Prayer

Father God, we thank you for this wonderful planet and we pray that we will be good caretakers, sharing what we have with others.
Amen.

You're a fine one to talk!

Aim To show that you can't judge a book by its cover! Sometimes we judge people by what they wear or whether they are rich or poor.

Songs V.I.P. (*Come On, Let's Celebrate*)
Nobody's a nobody (*Come On, Let's Celebrate*)
Be kind and compassionate (*Bible Explosion*)
Jesus went out of his way (*Bible Explosion*)

Puppet sketch

(Micky comes out full of life but John has a stern face)

Micky	What's up!
John	What's up! Did you say what's up? What do you think is up!!?
Micky	Are you cross with me?
John	Am I cross with you? Did you ask if I am cross with you? Of course I am!
Micky	Why?
John	What do you mean, why? *(To audience)* Last week I was really proud of Micky. You see, his school had chosen him to run as part of a relay team in an inter-school sports day!
Micky	I was very pleased to be chosen too.
John	Micky's trainers were old and had holes so we spent last Saturday going round the shops and bought him some new ones!
Micky	Yes, they were very smart!
John	But when Micky lined up ready for the race I realised he wasn't wearing his new trainers – in fact he wasn't wearing any trainers!
Micky	Yes, that's true, and it did hurt my feet running round the hard track!
John	Yes, you were a lot slower than normal and came last! Why didn't you tell me if you'd lost your trainers.
Micky	I hadn't lost them!
John	Have they been stolen?
Micky	No!
John	Were they uncomfortable? Is that why you chose not to wear them?
Micky	No. They were the most comfortable trainers I've ever had!

Children's talks with puppet sketches 2

John	Then what? And it had better be good because I'm very cross with you. You let your team down! In fact you let the school down! In fact, you let me down!
Micky	Oh! I hadn't realised. I saw a boy – a boy I knew – who was being picked on by some other boys. They were laughing at him because of his trainers!
John	Why?
Micky	They were odd! His trainers weren't a pair!
John	What?
Micky	That's why everyone was calling him names.
John	That's a shame!
Micky	So I chased the boys off.
John	Right!
Micky	I know that his mum has had a hard time recently and they haven't got much money and I found myself saying: 'Here, you can have mine.'
John	Your what?
Micky	Trainers!
John	(*In an angry voice*) What! You've given your brand new trainers away!
Micky	Er . . . yes!
John	(*In a quieter voice*) Oh, Micky . . . (*Pause*) I'm proud of you! You did the right thing! Sorry I judged you unfairly! You weren't wearing your brand new trainers because you had given them to someone in need! Well done, Micky!

Bible story

Matthew 7:1-5 – Jesus said: 'Do not judge others!'

We sometimes look at other people and say: 'They're no good,' or 'They are rubbish,' or 'They are not as good as me.'

We sometimes think this because we don't like what they look like or where they are from! We judge them unfairly!

Jesus told a story about not judging others, but it's very short in the Bible, so here's a slightly different one instead:

One day a boy was walking down the street. He stopped to watch a carpenter working. The carpenter was sawing a piece of wood when, suddenly, a cloud of sawdust blew up and covered the little boy.

'Ouch!' he cried. 'My eyes are sore.' He started to rub them and they started to run.

Because of the water in his eyes he struggled to see some lads as they came across to him. They had seen what had happened but rather than trying to help him they just started to laugh.

'Look at him – his eyes are running. Is that sawdust in your eyes? How embarrassing, I wouldn't be seen dead having sawdust in my eyes!'

The boy looked up to see who was being so cruel and as he did he noticed that they looked rather odd themselves! They hadn't got a tiny piece of sawdust in their eyes like he had, but a big plank of wood sticking out, which kept knocking into things.

Who do you think looked the most odd? The boy with the tiny specks of sawdust that you couldn't even see, or the lads with great big planks of wood sticking out of their eyes?

The lads were judging the boy because he had the sawdust in his eyes, but they were in a bigger mess than he was!

Round-up

Find one of your favourite books and put a new, dull cover on it. Get some more books that have bright covers. Ask a volunteer which book they would choose to read. Then show them which one is your favourite. We often judge people before we really know anything about them or their situation.

Prayer

Lord, thank you that we are all unique and different from one another! Help us not to judge other people, thinking that they are not as good as us. Thank you that we are all equal in your eyes.
Amen.

Resources

John Hardwick

John Hardwick travels widely and is available for:
- cool and crazy praise parties
- training sessions on creative communication
- day presentations in primary schools
- all-age worship celebrations.

He also has other publications such as CDs and videos.
Check him out at <**www.johnhardwick.org.uk**>
Office Tel: 01223 519489
e-mail: johnhardwick36@hotmail.com

Music

Songs used in this book can be found in:
Come On, Let's Celebrate CD and music book, complete with children's talks, by John Hardwick (Books 1 and 2 published by Kevin Mayhew Ltd)
Bible Explosion CD and Music Pack <**www.johnhardwick.org.uk**>
There is also a great selection of songs in:
Kidsource – super songs for church and school (Kevin Mayhew Ltd, Buxhall, Stowmarket, Suffolk IP14 3BW. Tel: 01449 737978. Fax: 01449 737834)
<**www.kevinmayhew.com**>
Full range of children's books and resources.

Puppet Suppliers

Children Worldwide – Full range of puppets.
Children Worldwide, Dalesdown, Honeybridge Lane, Dial Post, Horsham, West Sussex RH13 8NX. Tel: 01403 711032
<**www.childrenworldwide.org.uk**>

One Way UK – A full range of puppets.
One Way UK, Unit D1, Acre Business Park, Acre Road, Reading RG2 0SA
Tel: 0845 490 1929
<**www.onewayuk.com**>
e-mail: info@onewayuk.com

Useful
websites

<*www.gsuslive.co.uk*>
An organisation which has a mobile trailer designed for use in school. An interactive and exciting programme aiming to bring RE to life!

<www.request.org.uk>
Re:Quest is an organisation that has a great selection of resources, and their website even includes a page where you can witness a baptism. This site also allows you to find out about different styles of churches, discovering more about the way they worship and what they believe.

<www.countiesuk.org>
An organisation that helps support Christian workers (including John Hardwick) and initiatives across the UK. Also produces '*Wow Factor*' Bible exhibitions.

<www.childrenworldwide.org.uk>
Has more than 40 children's workers across the UK.

<www.scriptureunion.org>
More than 40 school workers and evangelists across the UK.